NINJA DUAL ZONE AIR FRYER UK COOKBOOK FOR BEGINNERS

1200 Days Easy-to-Follow and Time-Saving Recipes to Unlock the Mysteries Of The Culinary World

SARA T. JONES

Copyright© 2023 By Sara T. Jones Rights Reserved

This book is copyright protected. It is only for personal use. You cannot amend, distribute, sell, use, quote or paraphrase any part of the content within this book, without the consent of the author or publisher.

Under no circumstances will any blame or legal responsibility be held against the publisher, or author, for any damages, reparation, or monetary loss due to the information contained within this book, either directly or indirectly.

Disclaimer Notice:

Please note the information contained within this document is for educational and entertainment purposes only. All effort has been executed to present accurate, up to date, reliable, complete information. No warranties of any kind are declared or implied. Readers acknowledge that the author is not engaged in the rendering of legal, financial, medical or professional advice. The content within this book has been derived from various sources. Please consult a licensed professional before attempting any techniques outlined in this book.

By reading this document, the reader agrees that under no circumstances is the author responsible for any losses, direct or indirect, that are incurred as a result of the use of the information contained within this document, including, but not limited to, errors, omissions, or inaccuracies.

EDITOR: LYN	INTERIOR DESIGN: FAIZAN
COVER ART: ABR	FOOD STYLIST: JO

Table of Contents

Introduction	1
Chapter 1	
Brief overview of the Ninja Dual Zone Air Fryer	2
What the Ninja Foodi Dual Zone Air Fryer Is	3
Basic Features and Functions	3
Advantages of Using the Ninja Dual Zone Air Fryer	5
Chapter 2	
Getting Started with the Ninja Dual Zone Air Fryer	6
Unboxing and Assembly	7
Tips for Getting the Most Out of Your Air Fryer	7
Maintaining and Cleaning the Appliance	8
Air Fryer Cooking Chart	10
Chapter 3	
Bread and Breakfast Recipes	12
Goat Cheese, Beet, And Kale Frittata	13
Chicken Saltimbocca Sandwiches	13
Jalapeño Egg Cups	13
Bacon And Cheese Quiche	13
Air Fried Sausage	14
Bacon Quiche Tarts	14
Egg & Spinach Pizza	14
Cheese Eggs And Leeks	14
Pepper Egg Cups	15
Baked Porridge	15
Eggnog Bread	16
Breakfast Bacon	16
Onion Marinated Skirt Steak	16
Chapter 4	
Appetizers and Snacks Recipes	17
Homemade Chips	18
Bacon-Wrapped Cheese Sticks	18
Fried Pineapple Chunks	18
Banana Muffin	19
Roasted Peanuts	19
Carrot Cake	19
Bacon-Wrapped Onion Rings	20
Banana And Rice Pudding	20
Simple Butter Cake	20
Broiled Grapefruit	21
Spicy Cheese-Stuffed Mushrooms	21
Coconut And Berries Cream	21
Cream Cheese Shortbread Cookies	22
Cinnamon-Sugar Pretzel Bites	22
Chapter 5	
Fish and Seafood Recipes	23
Crumb-Topped Sole	24
Teriyaki Salmon	24
Honey Glazed Salmon	25
Super Crunchy Flounder Fillets	25
Tilapia with Garlic and Lemon	26
Potato Chip-crusted Cod	26
Lemon Pepper Salmon	26
Crispy Catfish	26

Spicy Cod Fillets	27
Garlicky Sea Bass With Root Veggies	27
Basil Crab Cakes With Fresh Salad	27
Horseradish-Crusted Salmon Fillets	28
Bacon-Wrapped Cajun Scallops	28
Butternut Squash-Wrapped Halibut Fillets	28
Prawn Skewers	29
Lemon-Dill Salmon With Green Beans	29
Garlic-Lemon Steamer Clams	29
Simple Sesame Squid On The Grill	29
Chinese Firecracker Shrimp	30
Seared Scallops In Beurre Blanc	30
Breaded Tilapia	30
Nacho Chips Crusted Prawns	31
Pecan-Crusted Tilapia	31
Lemon-Roasted Salmon Fillets	31
Crunchy Flounder Gratin	31

Chapter 6
Poultry Mains Recipes — 32

Fajita Stuffed Chicken	33
Almond Chicken	33
Gingered Chicken Drumsticks	34
Southern Style Chicken	34
Garlicky Duck Legs	34
Yummy Stuffed Chicken Breast	34
Tuscan Stuffed Chicken	35
Family Chicken Fingers	35
Chicken Tenders With Basil-strawberry Glaze	35
Spinach And Feta Stuffed Chicken Breasts	36
Teriyaki Chicken Legs	36
Stuffed Chicken Breasts	36
Rosemary Turkey Legs	37
Peppery Lemon-chicken Breast	37
Mushroom & Turkey Bread Pizza	37
Lemon Pepper Chicken Wings	38
Mumbai Chicken Nuggets	38
Southern-fried Chicken Livers	39
Chicken Burgers With Blue Cheese Sauce	39
Turkey Tenderloin With A Lemon Touch	40
Chicken Cordon Bleu	40

Chapter 7
Beef, Pork & Lamb Recipes — 41

Simple BBQ Baby Pork Ribs	42
Simple Lamb Loin Chops	42
T-bone Steak With Roasted Tomato, Corn And Asparagus Salsa	42
Filet Mignon Wrapped in Bacon	43
Taco Seasoned Steak	43
Crispy Pierogi With Kielbasa And Onions	43
Honey Mesquite Pork Chops	44
Air Fried Steak	44
Lemon-Butter Veal Cutlets	44
Marinated Rib-Eye Steak With Herb Roasted Mushrooms	45
Kielbasa Sausage with Pineapple and Peppers	45
Hot Dogs Wrapped in Bacon	46
Pork Belly Marinated In Onion-coconut Cream	46
Italian Meatballs	46
Greek-style Pork Stuffed Jalapeño Poppers	47
Sweet Potato-Crusted Pork Rib Chops	47
Bacon Wrapped Filets Mignons	48
California Burritos	48

Chapter 8
Vegetarians Recipes — 49

Pepper-Pineapple With Butter-Sugar Glaze	50
Baked Polenta With Chili-cheese	50
Twice-Baked Broccoli-Cheddar Potatoes	51
Italian Seasoned Easy Pasta Chips	51
Home-Style Cinnamon Rolls	52
Charred Cauliflower Tacos	52
Chicano Rice Bowls	53
Brussels Sprouts With Balsamic Oil	53
Spicy Sesame Tempeh Slaw With Peanut Dressing	54
Sweet And Spicy Barbecue Tofu	54
Mushroom Bolognese Casserole	55
Meatless Kimchi Bowls	55
Rigatoni With Roasted Onions, Fennel, Spinach And Lemon Pepper Ricotta	55

Chapter 9
Vegetable Side Dishes Recipes — 56

Grilled Cheese	57
Caraway Seed Pretzel Sticks	57
Zucchini Fries	58
Roasted Asparagus	58
Balsamic Green Beans With Bacon	59
Cheesy Potato Pot	59
Tandoori Cauliflower	60
Steakhouse Baked Potatoes	60
Asparagus & Cherry Tomato Roast	61
Perfect Asparagus	61
Mouth-Watering Provençal Mushrooms	62
Chili-Oiled Brussels Sprouts	62
Sriracha Green Beans	62
Panzanella Salad With Crispy Croutons	63
Perfect Chips	63

Chapter 10
Holiday Specials — 64

Lush Snack Mix	65
Mushroom and Green Bean Casserole	65
Hasselback Potatoes	66
Mexican Pizza	66
Teriyaki Prawn Skewers	67
Thick-Crust Pepperoni Pizza	67
Air Fried Blistered Tomatoes	68
Honey Glazed BBQ Pork Ribs	68
Classic Churros	69
Fried Dill Pickles with Buttermilk Dressing	69
Prawns with Sriracha and Worcestershire Sauce	70
Simple Lamb Meatballs	70
Golden Nuggets	71
Air Fried Spicy Olives	71
Cinnamon Rolls with Cream Glaze	72
Cajun Flank Steak	72
Jewish Blintzes	73
Kale Salad Sushi Rolls with Sriracha Mayonnaise	73

Appendix 1 Measurement Conversion Chart	**74**
Appendix 2 The Dirty Dozen and Clean Fifteen	**75**
Appendix 3 Index	**76**

Introduction

Air fryers are kitchen appliances that use hot air to cook food, providing a crispy, fried texture without the need for oil. They have become increasingly popular in recent years due to their ability to cook food quickly and healthily, making them an excellent alternative to traditional frying methods.

Air fryers work by using a heating element and a fan to circulate hot air around the food, providing a crispy texture on the outside while keeping the inside moist and tender. They can be used to cook a variety of foods, including chicken, fish, vegetables, and even desserts, making them a versatile and convenient kitchen appliance.

One of the main benefits of using an air fryer is that it allows you to cook food with less oil than traditional frying methods. This makes air frying a healthier option, as it can reduce the amount of fat and calories in your food. Additionally, air fryers are also easy to use, with simple controls and a digital display that makes it easy to select your cooking settings and monitor your progress.

Another benefit of air fryers is that they can save you time in the kitchen. They can cook food faster than traditional frying methods, and some models even have pre-programmed settings for specific foods, allowing you to cook your favorite dishes with just the push of a button.

Chapter 1: Brief overview of the Ninja Dual Zone Air Fryer

What the Ninja Foodi Dual Zone Air Fryer Is

The Ninja Foodi Dual Zone Air Fryer is a kitchen appliance that combines the functions of an air fryer with a second cooking compartment that allows for simultaneous cooking of two different foods at two different temperatures. The air fryer function uses hot air to circulate around the food, providing a crispy, fried texture without the need for oil. The second cooking compartment can be used for other cooking methods, such as roasting, baking, or dehydrating. This dual-zone feature allows for flexibility and convenience in cooking multiple dishes at once, without having to use multiple appliances or wait for one dish to finish before starting another.

The Ninja Foodi Dual Zone Air Fryer has indeed revolutionized kitchen technology by providing users with a convenient, versatile, and healthier way of cooking their favorite foods. With its advanced features and innovative design, this kitchen appliance has become a must-have for those who value convenience, speed, and taste.

One of the most significant advantages of the Ninja Foodi Dual Zone Air Fryer is its ability to cook food quickly and efficiently. The hot air circulates around the food, providing a crispy, golden exterior while sealing in the moisture, resulting in juicy and flavorful food that is not only delicious but also healthier than traditional frying methods. The dual-zone feature allows for simultaneous cooking of two different foods at two different temperatures, providing users with the flexibility and convenience they need to cook multiple dishes at once.

The Ninja Foodi Dual Zone Air Fryer is also incredibly easy to use, with simple controls and a digital display that makes it easy to select your cooking settings and monitor your progress. The smart technology built into the appliance ensures that your food is cooked perfectly every time, eliminating the need for guesswork and making it easy to achieve consistent results.

Furthermore, the Ninja Foodi Dual Zone Air Fryer is also easy to clean and maintain, with removable parts that can be washed in the dishwasher. Its compact design and sleek appearance make it an attractive addition to any kitchen, while its ability to cook a wide range of foods, from meats and vegetables to desserts, provide users with endless recipe ideas and meal possibilities.

Basic Features and Functions

Here are the features of the Ninja Foodi Dual Zone Air Fryer:

DUAL ZONE COOKING
The Ninja Foodi Dual Zone Air Fryer has two independent cooking zones that can be used at the same time, allowing

you to cook two different foods with different temperatures and times. For example, you could cook chicken in one zone and french fries in the other. The dual zones have a combined capacity of 6.5 quarts.

AIR FRY, ROAST, REHEAT, AND DEHYDRATE

The Ninja Foodi Dual Zone Air Fryer has four cooking functions. The air fry function uses hot air to fry food without using oil, making it a healthier option. The roast function is great for cooking meats, providing a crispy exterior and juicy interior. The reheat function warms up leftovers quickly and efficiently. The dehydrate function removes moisture from foods, making it possible to make dried fruits or beef jerky.

SMART FINISH TECHNOLOGY

The Ninja Foodi Dual Zone Air Fryer has Smart Finish Technology that automatically stops cooking when the food is done. This prevents overcooking and ensures that the food is cooked to perfection. The feature is available for both cooking zones.

DIGITAL DISPLAY

The Ninja Foodi Dual Zone Air Fryer has a digital display that shows the cooking temperature, time, and selected cooking function. The display is easy to read and provides real-time updates, making it easy to monitor your cooking progress and make adjustments as needed.

DISHWASHER-SAFE PARTS

The removable parts of the Ninja Foodi Dual Zone Air Fryer, such as the cooking baskets, crisper plates, and racks, are dishwasher safe. This makes cleanup quick and easy.

LARGE CAPACITY

The Ninja Foodi Dual Zone Air Fryer has a large capacity, allowing you to cook for a crowd or make multiple dishes at once. The two independent cooking zones have a combined capacity of 6.5 quarts, which is enough to cook a 5-pound chicken or 3 pounds of french fries.

CUSTOMIZABLE COOKING SETTINGS

The Ninja Foodi Dual Zone Air Fryer allows you to customize the cooking settings for each cooking zone. You can choose from 5 different levels of doneness for each zone, from rare to well done, ensuring that your food is cooked exactly the way you want it.

DELAY START AND KEEP WARM

The Ninja Foodi Dual Zone Air Fryer has a delay start function that allows you to start cooking at a later time, and a keep warm function that keeps the food warm until you're ready to serve it.

Here are the functions of the ninja foodi dual zone air fryer:

AIR FRY FUNCTION

The air fry function of the Ninja Foodi Dual Zone Air Fryer uses hot air to fry food without using oil, making it a healthier option. This function can be used to cook a variety of foods, such as chicken wings, fries, and even vegetables. For example, the Ninja Foodi Dual Zone Air Fryer can cook 3 pounds of french fries in one cooking zone while cooking chicken wings in the other, both with perfect crispiness.

ROAST FUNCTION

The roast function of the Ninja Foodi Dual Zone Air Fryer is great for cooking meats, providing a crispy exterior and juicy interior. This function can be used to cook a variety of meats, such as pork roast, beef roast, and even a whole chicken. For example, the Ninja Foodi Dual Zone Air Fryer can cook a 5-pound chicken in one cooking zone while cooking a beef roast in the other, both with perfect doneness.

REHEAT FUNCTION

The reheat function of the Ninja Foodi Dual Zone Air Fryer warms up leftovers quickly and efficiently, making them taste like they were just cooked. This function can be used to reheat a variety of foods, such as pizza, chicken, and even fish. For example, the Ninja Foodi Dual Zone Air Fryer can reheat a slice of pizza in one cooking zone while cooking chicken wings in the other, both with perfect texture.

DEHYDRATE FUNCTION

The dehydrate function of the Ninja Foodi Dual Zone Air Fryer removes moisture from foods, making it possible to make dried fruits or beef jerky. This function can be used to dehydrate a variety of foods, such as fruits, vegetables, and even herbs. For example, the Ninja Foodi Dual Zone Air Fryer can dehydrate apples in one cooking zone while dehydrating bananas in the other, both with perfect crispiness.

Advantages of Using the Ninja Dual Zone Air Fryer

HEALTHIER COOKING

One of the main advantages of using the Ninja Foodi Dual Zone Air Fryer is that it allows you to cook food with little to no oil. The air fry function uses hot air to cook food, creating a crispy texture on the outside while keeping the inside tender and juicy. This is a healthier option compared to traditional deep-frying methods, which require a lot of oil that can make food high in fat and calories. With the Ninja Foodi Dual Zone Air Fryer, you can enjoy your favorite fried foods, such as chicken wings or french fries, with less guilt.

VERSATILITY

Another advantage of the Ninja Foodi Dual Zone Air Fryer is its versatility. It offers multiple cooking functions, such as air fry, roast, reheat, and dehydrate. This means that you can use it to cook a variety of dishes, from roasted vegetables and meats to dried fruits and jerky. With the Ninja Foodi Dual Zone Air Fryer, you can replace several other kitchen gadgets, such as a dehydrator, toaster oven, or even a regular oven.

TIME-SAVING

The Ninja Foodi Dual Zone Air Fryer is a fast and efficient appliance that can cook food in a fraction of the time it takes with traditional cooking methods. The air fry function, for example, can cook food in as little as 20 minutes, compared to 45 minutes or more for traditional oven baking. With the Dual Zone technology, you can even cook two different foods simultaneously, saving even more time. This makes the Ninja Foodi Dual Zone Air Fryer a great option for busy people who want to cook healthy meals quickly and easily.

EASY TO USE AND CLEAN

The Ninja Foodi Dual Zone Air Fryer is easy to operate and clean. It has a user-friendly control panel that allows you to select the cooking function, time, and temperature with ease. The components of the Ninja Foodi Dual Zone Air Fryer are also dishwasher-safe, making cleaning up a breeze. The non-stick interior of the appliance also makes it easy to wipe clean with a damp cloth.

SPACE-SAVING

The Ninja Foodi Dual Zone Air Fryer has a compact design, making it a great space-saving option for smaller kitchens or apartments. It can fit easily on a countertop or in a cabinet, and its multi-functionality means that you can eliminate the need for several other kitchen appliances.

CONSISTENT RESULTS

The precision cooking technology of the Ninja Foodi Dual Zone Air Fryer ensures consistent results every time, giving you perfectly cooked food with crisp and juicy texture. The appliance has a digital timer and temperature control that allows you to set the cooking parameters accurately, ensuring that your food is cooked to perfection every time. This makes the Ninja Foodi Dual Zone Air Fryer a reliable and consistent cooking appliance that you can count on.

Chapter 2: Getting Started with the Ninja Dual Zone Air Fryer

Unboxing and Assembly

UNBOXING:

1. The Ninja Foodi Dual Zone Air Fryer comes in a large box that contains the appliance and its accessories. The box should be labeled with the model name and number, and should indicate that the contents are fragile and should be handled with care.
2. Carefully open the box and remove all the components, making sure not to damage them. The components should be wrapped in plastic and/or foam to protect them during shipping. It is important to inspect each component carefully to ensure that there is no damage or missing pieces.
3. Check that all the components are present and in good condition. The box should contain the air fryer base, cooking pot, air fry basket, crumb tray, control panel, and power cord.
4. Read the instruction manual carefully before assembling and using the appliance. The manual should contain important safety information, assembly instructions, and cooking tips.

ASSEMBLY:

1. Place the appliance on a flat and stable surface, making sure that it is in a well-ventilated area. The air fryer should be placed on a heat-resistant surface, away from walls, cabinets, and other heat-sensitive materials. The appliance should not be used near flammable materials or on a surface that is not stable.
2. Insert the crumb tray at the bottom of the appliance. The crumb tray collects any food particles that fall during cooking and makes cleaning up easier.
3. Attach the cooking pot to the crumb tray, making sure that it clicks into place. The cooking pot is where you will place the food you want to cook.
4. Attach the control panel to the top of the appliance, making sure that it is securely in place. The control panel is where you will select the cooking mode, temperature, and time.
5. Attach the air fry basket to the cooking pot, making sure that it is inserted correctly. The air fry basket is where you will place the food you want to air fry.
6. If using the second cooking zone, attach the cooking pot and air fry basket to the other side of the appliance. The Ninja Foodi Dual Zone Air Fryer has two separate cooking zones that can be used at the same time to cook different foods.
7. Plug in the power cord and turn on the appliance to start using it. Once the appliance is plugged in, you can turn it on by pressing the power button on the control panel.

It is important to follow the assembly instructions carefully to ensure that the appliance is set up correctly and safely. The Ninja Foodi Dual Zone Air Fryer is designed to be easy to assemble and use, so you should be able to start cooking with it in no time.

Tips for Getting the Most Out of Your Air Fryer

PREHEAT THE AIR FRYER

Just like with an oven, preheating your air fryer can help ensure that your food cooks evenly and comes out crispy. Most air fryers have a preheat function or can be preheated manually for a few minutes before adding the food.

DON'T OVERCROWD THE BASKET

It can be tempting to pack as much food as possible into the air fryer basket, but this can actually hinder the cooking process. Overcrowding can lead to uneven cooking and steaming rather than air frying. Make sure to leave enough space between the food items for air to circulate and cook evenly.

USE A LIGHT COATING OF OIL

While air fryers are designed to cook food without the need for oil, using a light coating of oil can help the food crisp up and develop a golden brown color. Use a cooking oil spray or lightly brush the food with oil before cooking.

SHAKE THE BASKET

During cooking, pause the cooking process and shake the basket to ensure that the food is cooked evenly on all sides. This will also help prevent any sticking and allow the excess oil or moisture to drip down.

EXPERIMENT WITH DIFFERENT FOODS

Air fryers are versatile appliances that can be used to cook a variety of foods, from vegetables and meats to desserts and snacks. Don't be afraid to experiment with different recipes and food combinations to discover new and exciting dishes.

CLEAN THE AIR FRYER REGULARLY

Keeping your air fryer clean is essential for maintaining its performance and prolonging its lifespan. Most air fryer components are dishwasher safe or can be cleaned with a damp cloth and mild soap. Make sure to clean the basket, cooking pot, and control panel regularly to prevent buildup and maintain the appliance's performance.

Maintaining and Cleaning the Appliance

UNPLUG THE APPLIANCE

Always unplug the air fryer before cleaning it to avoid any electrical hazards.

WAIT FOR THE APPLIANCE TO COOL DOWN

Allow the air fryer to cool down completely before cleaning it. Attempting to clean it while it is still hot can cause burns or damage the appliance.

REMOVE THE COOKING POT AND BASKET

Take out the cooking pot and basket from the air fryer and wash them in warm soapy water. You can also clean them in the dishwasher if they are dishwasher safe, but make sure to check the manufacturer's instructions first.

WIPE THE EXTERIOR

Wipe the exterior of the air fryer with a damp cloth and mild soap. Avoid using abrasive cleaners or scouring pads, as they can scratch the surface of the appliance.

CLEAN THE HEATING ELEMENT

Use a soft brush or cloth to clean the heating element of any food debris or residue. Be careful not to touch the heating element directly as it can be hot.

CHECK THE AIR VENTS

Make sure to check the air vents for any dust or debris that may have accumulated. Use a soft brush or cloth to remove any dirt from the vents.

STORE THE APPLIANCE PROPERLY

Store the air fryer in a dry and cool place, and make sure to cover it to prevent dust and debris from entering.

AVOID USING HARSH CHEMICALS

Do not use harsh chemicals such as bleach or ammonia to clean your air fryer, as they can damage the appliance and leave a strong odor or residue.

USE BAKING SODA TO REMOVE STAINS

If there are stubborn stains or food residue on the cooking pot or basket, mix baking soda with water to create a paste. Apply the paste to the affected areas and let it sit for 10-15 minutes before wiping it off with a damp cloth.

CLEAN THE AIR FRYER REGULARLY

It is important to clean your air fryer after every use to prevent the buildup of grease and food residue. Refer to the manufacturer's instructions for specific cleaning and maintenance instructions for your air fryer.

In conclusion, the Ninja Dual Zone Air Fryer is a revolutionary kitchen appliance that has transformed the way we cook and enjoy our favorite foods. With its unique features and functions, it allows for quick and healthy cooking with little to no oil, resulting in delicious and crispy meals every time.

Through this book, we have explored the various features and functions of the Ninja Dual Zone Air Fryer, as well as provided tips and tricks for getting the most out of your appliance. From unboxing and assembly to cleaning and maintenance, we have covered all the important aspects of using and caring for your air fryer.

We hope that this book has provided you with valuable insights and information on the Ninja Dual Zone Air Fryer, and that you will enjoy using this amazing appliance for many years to come. Happy cooking!

Air Fryer Cooking Chart

Food	Temperature (°C)	Cooking Time (minutes)
French fries (thin)	200	10-15
French fries (thick)	200	15-20
Chicken wings	180	20-25
Chicken breast	180	15-20
Salmon fillet	200	8-10
Shrimp	200	8-10
Onion rings	200	8-10
Vegetables (broccoli, etc.)	180	10-15
Frozen vegetables (mix)	180	10-15
Breaded fish fillets	200	10-12
Hamburgers	200	8-10
Bacon	180	6-8
Sausages	180	12-15
Meatballs	180	12-15
Baked potatoes	200	45-50
Sweet potatoes	200	20-25
Chicken breasts	200	15-20 min
Chicken thighs	200	20-25 min
Chicken wings	200	18-20 min
Fish fillets	200	8-12 min
Shrimp	200	6-8 min
Scallops	200	6-8 min
Salmon	200	10-12 min
Pork chops	200	12-15 min
Pork tenderloin	200	20-25 min
Steak (1 inch thick)	200	8-10 min
Hamburger patties	200	8-10 min
Hot dogs/sausages	200	6-8 min
French fries	200	15-20 min
Sweet potato fries	200	15-20 min
Potato wedges	200	15-20 min
Onion rings	200	12-15 min
Zucchini/squash fries	200	10-12 min
Broccoli/cauliflower	200	8-10 min
Brussel sprouts	200	12-15 min
Carrots	200	12-15 min
Asparagus	200	6-8 min

Food	Temperature (°C)	Cooking Time (minutes)
Corn on the cob	200	12-15 min
Baked potatoes	200	40-45 min
Stuffed mushrooms	200	8-10 min
Roasted peppers	200	8-10 min
Chicken nuggets	200	10-12 min
Meatballs	200	10-12 min
Spring rolls	200	10-12 min
Mozzarella sticks	200	6-8 min
Jalapeno poppers	200	8-10 min
Quiche	180	25-30 min
Puff pastry	200	10-12 min
Apple turnovers	200	12-15 min
Chocolate chip cookies	180	6-8 min

Note: Cooking times may vary depending on the type and brand of air fryer, as well as the size and thickness of the food being cooked. Always refer to the manufacturer's instructions and use a food thermometer to ensure that food is cooked to a safe temperature.

Chapter 3
Bread and Breakfast Recipes

Goat Cheese, Beet, And Kale Frittata

Prep time: 5 minutes | Cook time: 20 minutes | Serves 6

- 6 large eggs
- ½ teaspoon garlic powder
- ¼ teaspoon black pepper
- ¼ teaspoon salt
- 1 cup chopped kale
- 1 cup cooked and chopped red beets
- ⅓ cup crumbled goat cheese

1. Preheat the air fryer to 320°F (160°C).
2. In a medium bowl, whisk the eggs with the garlic powder, pepper, and salt. Mix in the kale, beets, and goat cheese.
3. Spray an oven-safe 7-inch springform pan with cooking spray. Pour the egg mixture into the pan and place it in the air fryer basket.
4. Cook for 20 minutes, or until the internal temperature reaches 73°C (145°F).
5. When the frittata is cooked, let it set for 5 minutes before removing from the pan.
6. Slice and serve immediately.

Chicken Saltimbocca Sandwiches

Prep time: 5 minutes | Cook time: 11 minutes | Serves 3

- 3 5-6 oz boneless, skinless chicken breasts
- 6 thin slices of Parma ham
- 6 slices of Provolone cheese
- 3 long soft rolls, such as ciabatta or baguette, split open lengthwise
- 3 tbsp pesto, purchased or homemade

1. Preheat the air fryer to 200°C/400°F.
2. Wrap each chicken breast with 2 slices of Parma ham, spiraling the ham around the breast and overlapping the slices a bit to cover the breast. The Parma ham will stick to the chicken more readily than bacon does.
3. When the air fryer is at temperature, set the wrapped chicken breasts in the basket and air-fry undisturbed for 10 minutes or until the Parma ham is crisp and the chicken is cooked through.
4. Overlap 2 slices of Provolone cheese on each breast. Air-fry undisturbed for 1 minute or until melted. Take the basket out of the machine.
5. Spread the insides of the rolls with the pesto, then use kitchen tongs to place a wrapped and cheesy chicken breast in each roll.

Jalapeño Egg Cups

Prep time: 5 minutes | Cook time: 14 minutes | Serves 4

- 4 large eggs
- ½ teaspoon salt
- ¼ teaspoon ground black pepper
- ¼ cup chopped pickled jalapeños
- 2 ounces cream cheese, softened
- ¼ teaspoon garlic powder
- ½ cup shredded sharp Cheddar cheese

1. Grease four 4-inch ramekins with cooking spray. In a medium bowl, beat the eggs together with salt and pepper, then pour evenly into the ramekins.
2. In a separate large bowl, mix together the chopped jalapeños, cream cheese, garlic powder, and Cheddar cheese. Spoon 1/4 of the mixture into the center of each ramekin.
3. Place the ramekins in the air fryer basket. Set the temperature to 160°C (320°F) and the timer for 14 minutes. The eggs will be set when done. Serve warm.

Bacon And Cheese Quiche

Prep time: 5 minutes | Cook time: 12 minutes | Serves 2

- 3 large eggs
- 2 tablespoons heavy whipping cream
- ¼ teaspoon salt
- 4 slices cooked sugar-free bacon, crumbled
- ½ cup shredded mild Cheddar cheese

1. In a large bowl, whisk together eggs, cream, and salt until well combined. Stir in chopped bacon and grated Cheddar cheese.
2. Pour the mixture evenly into two ungreased 4-inch ramekins. Place the ramekins in the air fryer basket.
3. Set the air fryer temperature to 160°C and cook the quiches for 12 minutes, or until fluffy and set in the middle.
4. Let the quiches cool in the ramekins for 5 minutes before serving warm.

Air Fried Sausage

Prep time: 10 minutes | Cook time: 13 minutes | Serves 4

- 4 sausage links, raw and uncooked

1. Arrange the sausages in the air fryer basket.
2. Place the basket in the air fryer.
3. Select the Air Fry mode and set the temperature to 200 degrees Celsius and the time to 13 minutes.
4. Press the Start button to begin cooking.
5. Turn the sausages over halfway through cooking.
6. Once the sausages are cooked, remove them from the air fryer and serve hot.

Bacon Quiche Tarts

Prep time: 15 minutes | Cook time: 20 minutes | Serves 8

- 2 eggs
- 5 teaspoons milk
- 6 oz. cream cheese
- ½ cup grated cheddar cheese
- 1 tablespoon onion, chopped
- 2 tablespoons green bell pepper, chopped
- 8 oz. refrigerated shortcrust pastry, separated into triangles
- 5 rashers of back bacon, cooked and crumbled

1. Beat eggs in a bowl.
2. Stir in milk, cream cheese, cheddar cheese, onion, and green bell pepper.
3. Press shortcrust pastry triangles into muffin cups.
4. Add egg mixture to the muffin cups.
5. Sprinkle with bacon.
6. Place muffin cups inside the air fryer basket.
7. Choose bake setting.
8. Cook at 190°C for 20 minutes.

Egg & Spinach Pizza

Prep time: 20 minutes | Cook time: 15 minutes | Serves 4

- 1 ready-to-bake pizza crust
- 142 g (5 oz.) baby spinach
- 1 tablespoon olive oil
- 25 g (1/4 cup) grated Parmesan cheese
- 3 tablespoons sour cream
- 1 clove garlic, minced
- Salt and pepper to taste
- 4 eggs

1. Preheat the air fryer to 180°C (350°F).
2. Slice the pizza crust into 4 to fit inside the air fryer basket.
3. In a frying pan over medium heat, cook the baby spinach in the olive oil until wilted.
4. Add the cooked spinach to a bowl.
5. Stir in the grated Parmesan cheese, sour cream, minced garlic, and season with salt and pepper to taste.
6. Spread the spinach mixture evenly on top of the pizza crust.
7. Crack one egg on top of each pizza.
8. Place the pizza in the air fryer basket.
9. Set the temperature to 180°C (350°F) and bake for 10-12 minutes or until the egg whites are set and the yolks are cooked to your liking.
10. Serve hot.

Cheese Eggs And Leeks

Prep time: 5 minutes | Cook time: 7 minutes | Serves 2

- 2 leeks, chopped
- 4 eggs, whisked
- ¼ cup Cheddar cheese, shredded
- ½ cup Mozzarella cheese, shredded
- 1 teaspoon avocado oil

1. Preheat the air fryer to 200°C (400°F). Grease the air fryer basket with avocado oil.
2. In a mixing bowl, combine the chopped leeks, whisked eggs, Cheddar cheese, and Mozzarella cheese.
3. Pour the egg mixture into the air fryer basket and cook for 7 minutes or until the omelette is set.
4. Serve hot.

Pepper Egg Cups
Prep time: 15 minutes | Cook time: 18 minutes | Serves 4

- 2 halved bell pepper, seeds removed
- 4 eggs
- 1 teaspoon olive oil
- 1 pinch salt and black pepper
- 1 pinch chilli flakes

1. Preheat the air fryer to 180°C (356°F).
2. Slice the bell peppers in half, lengthwise, and remove their seeds and the inner portion to get a cup-like shape.
3. Rub olive oil on the edges of the bell peppers.
4. Crack 1 egg in each half of bell pepper.
5. Sprinkle salt, black pepper, and chilli flakes on top of the eggs.
6. Place the bell pepper halves in the air fryer basket.
7. Cook at 180°C (356°F) for 18 minutes.
8. Serve warm.

Baked Porridge
Prep time: 10 minutes | Cook time: 25 minutes | Serves 4

- 1 ½ cups rolled oats
- 1 egg, beaten
- ½ cup milk
- ¼ cup unsalted butter, melted
- ½ cup caster sugar
- 1 teaspoon baking powder
- 1 teaspoon vanilla extract
- ¾ teaspoon salt

1. In a mixing bowl, combine the rolled oats, beaten egg, milk, melted butter, caster sugar, baking powder, vanilla extract, and salt.
2. Stir until well combined.
3. Pour the mixture into an air fryer-safe baking dish.
4. Place the dish in the air fryer basket.
5. Set the air fryer to bake mode.
6. Cook at 350°F (180°C) for 25 minutes.
7. Once cooked, remove from the air fryer and allow it to cool for a few minutes before serving.

Eggnog Bread

Prep time: 10 minutes | Cook time: 18 minutes | Serves 6 to 8

- 235 ml flour, plus more for dusting
- 60 ml sugar
- 1 teaspoon baking powder
- ¼ teaspoon salt
- ¼ teaspoon nutmeg
- 120 ml eggnog
- 1 egg yolk
- 1 tablespoon plus 1 teaspoon butter, melted
- 60 ml pecans
- 60 ml chopped candied fruit (cherries, pineapple, or mixed fruits)
- Cooking spray

1. In a medium bowl, stir together the flour, sugar, baking powder, salt, and nutmeg.
2. Add eggnog, egg yolk, and butter. Mix well but do not beat.
3. Stir in nuts and fruit.
4. Spray a baking pan with cooking spray and dust with flour. Spread batter into prepared pan and place into the zone 1 drawer. Bake at 180°C for 18 minutes or until top is dark golden brown and bread starts to pull away from sides of pan.
5. Serve immediately.

Breakfast Bacon

Prep time: 10 minutes | Cook time: 14 minutes | Serves 4

- 225g bacon slices

1. Spread half of the bacon slices in each of the crisper plate evenly in a single layer.
2. Return the crisper plate to the Ninja Foodi Dual Zone Air Fryer.
3. Choose the Air Fry mode for Zone 1 and set the temperature to 200 degrees C and the time to 14 minutes.
4. Select the "MATCH" button to copy the settings for Zone 2.
5. Initiate cooking by pressing the START/STOP button.
6. Flip the crispy bacon once cooked halfway through, then resume cooking.
7. Serve.

Onion Marinated Skirt Steak

Prep time: 5 minutes | Cook time: 45 minutes | Serves 3

- 1 large red onion, grated or pureed
- 2 tablespoons brown sugar
- 1 tablespoon vinegar
- 680g skirt steak
- Salt and pepper to taste

1. Place all ingredients in a resealable bag and allow to marinate in the refrigerator for at least 2 hours.
2. Preheat the air fryer to 200°C/180°C fan/gas mark 6.
3. Place the grill pan accessory in the air fryer.
4. Grill for 15 minutes per batch.
5. Flip every 8 minutes for even grilling.
6. Serve hot.

Chapter 4
Appetizers and Snacks Recipes

Homemade Chips

Prep time: 5 minutes | Cook time: 25 minutes | Serves 2

- 2 to 3 russet potatoes, peeled and cut into ½-inch sticks
- 2 to 3 teaspoons olive or vegetable oil
- salt

1. Preheat the oven to 220°C/200°C fan/gas mark 7. Bring a large saucepan of salted water to a boil on the stovetop while you peel and cut the potatoes. Blanch the potatoes in the boiling salted water for 4 minutes. Strain the potatoes and rinse them with cold water. Dry them well with a clean kitchen towel.
2. Toss the dried potato chips gently with the oil and spread them out on a baking tray. Bake for 25-30 minutes, turning occasionally, until golden brown and crispy. Season the chips with salt midway through cooking and serve them hot with tomato ketchup, mayonnaise, or malt vinegar.

Bacon-Wrapped Cheese Sticks

Prep time: 5 minutes | Cook time: 12 minutes | Serves 6

- 6 sticks of mozzarella cheese
- 6 slices of streaky bacon

1. Place the mozzarella sticks on a medium plate, cover, and place into the freezer for 1 hour until frozen solid.
2. Wrap each mozzarella stick in 1 piece of streaky bacon and secure with a toothpick. Place the wrapped sticks onto a baking tray lined with parchment paper. Preheat the oven to 200°C/180°C fan/gas mark 6.
3. Bake for 12-15 minutes or until the bacon is crispy and the cheese is melted. Turn the sticks once during cooking to ensure they cook evenly.
4. Serve hot as a snack or appetizer.

Fried Pineapple Chunks

Prep time: 5 minutes | Cook time: 10 minutes | Serves 3

- 3 tablespoons Cornflour
- 1 Large egg white, beaten until frothy
- 1 cup Ground vanilla biscuit crumbs (not low-fat biscuits)
- ¼ teaspoon Ground dried ginger
- 18 Fresh 1-inch chunks peeled and cored pineapple

1. Preheat the air fryer to 200°C.
2. Put the cornflour in a medium or large bowl. Put the beaten egg white in a small bowl. Pour the biscuit crumbs and ground dried ginger into a large sealable bag, shaking it a bit to combine them.
3. Dump the pineapple chunks into the bowl with the cornflour. Toss and stir until well coated. Use your cleaned fingers or a large fork like a shovel to pick up a few pineapple chunks, shake off any excess cornflour, and put them in the bowl with the egg white. Stir gently, then pick them up and let any excess egg white slip back into the rest. Put them in the bag with the crumb mixture. Repeat the cornflour-then-egg process until all the pineapple chunks are in the bag. Seal the bag and shake gently, turning the bag this way and that, to coat the pieces well.
4. Set the coated pineapple chunks in the basket with as much air space between them as possible. Even a fraction of an inch will work, but they should not touch. Air-fry undisturbed for 10 minutes, or until golden brown and crisp.
5. Gently dump the contents of the basket onto a wire rack. Cool for at least 5 minutes or up to 15 minutes before serving.

Banana Muffin

Prep time: 10 minutes | Cook time: 25 minutes | Serves 8

- 280g self-raising flour
- 1 tsp baking powder
- 115g caster sugar
- 2 large ripe bananas, mashed
- 2 eggs, beaten
- 120ml milk
- 110g unsalted butter, melted
- 1 tsp vanilla extract

1. Preheat the air fryer to 160°C (320°F).
2. In a large bowl, sift together the flour and baking powder. Add the caster sugar and mix well.
3. In a separate bowl, mix together the mashed bananas, beaten eggs, milk, melted butter, and vanilla extract.
4. Add the wet mixture to the dry mixture and mix until just combined.
5. Spoon the batter into muffin cups, filling each about 2/3 full.
6. Place the muffin cups inside the air fryer basket and select the bake setting.
7. Cook at 160°C (320°F) for 25 minutes or until the muffins are golden brown and a toothpick inserted into the center comes out clean.
8. Allow the muffins to cool for a few minutes in the muffin cups before transferring them to a wire rack to cool completely. Serve and enjoy!

Roasted Peanuts

Prep time: 5 minutes | Cook time: 14 minutes | Serves 10

- 2½ cups raw peanuts
- 1 tablespoon olive oil
- Salt, as required

1. Preheat the oven to 160°C/320°F.
2. Spread the peanuts in a single layer on a baking tray.
3. Roast the peanuts in the preheated oven for about 10 minutes, stirring occasionally.
4. Remove the peanuts from the oven and transfer them to a bowl.
5. Add the vegetable oil and salt to the bowl and toss to coat the peanuts evenly.
6. Return the peanuts to the baking tray and roast them for another 4 minutes.
7. Once done, transfer the hot nuts in a glass or steel bowl and serve.

Carrot Cake

Prep time: 10 minutes | Cook time: 15 minutes | Serves 6

- 1 carrot cake mix
- 2 large eggs
- 2/3 cup vegetable oil
- 1/2 cup water

1. In a mixing bowl, combine the carrot cake mix, eggs, vegetable oil, and water. Mix until smooth.
2. Pour the batter into a greased air fryer cake pan.
3. Preheat the air fryer to 320°F (160°C) for 5 minutes.
4. Place the cake pan in the air fryer basket and cook for 15 minutes.
5. Once done, remove the cake pan from the air fryer and let it cool on a wire rack.
6. Once the cake has cooled, slice it and serve.

Bacon-Wrapped Onion Rings

Prep time: 5 minutes | Cook time:10 minutes |Serves 8

- 1 large white onion, peeled and cut into 16 (¼"-thick) slices
- 8 rashers of streaky bacon

1. Preheat the oven to 200°C/400°F.
2. Stack 2 slices of onion and wrap with 1 rasher of bacon. Secure with a toothpick. Repeat with remaining onion slices and bacon.
3. Place the bacon-wrapped onion rings on a baking tray lined with parchment paper.
4. Roast the onion rings in the preheated oven for about 8-10 minutes, turning the rings halfway through cooking, until the bacon is crispy.
5. Once done, remove the toothpicks and serve the onion rings warm.

Banana And Rice Pudding

Prep time: 5 minutes | Cook time:20 minutes |Serves 6

- 175g pudding rice
- 700ml whole milk
- 2 ripe bananas, mashed
- 120ml maple syrup
- 1 teaspoon vanilla extract

1. Place all the ingredients in a pan that fits your air fryer; stir well.
2. Put the pan in the fryer and cook at 180°C for 20 minutes.
3. Stir the pudding, divide into cups, refrigerate, and serve cold.

Simple Butter Cake

Prep time: 25 minutes | Cook time: 20 minutes | Serves 8

- 235 ml plain flour
- 1¼ teaspoons baking powder
- ¼ teaspoon salt
- 120 ml plus 1½ tablespoons granulated white sugar
- 9½ tablespoons butter, at room temperature
- 2 large eggs
- 1 large egg yolk
- 2½ tablespoons milk
- 1 teaspoon vanilla extract
- Cooking spray

1. Spritz a cake pan with cooking spray.
2. Combine the flour, baking powder, and salt in a large bowl. Stir to mix well. Whip the sugar and butter in a separate bowl with a hand mixer on medium speed for 3 minutes.
3. Whip the eggs, egg yolk, milk, and vanilla extract into the sugar and butter mix with a hand mixer.
4. Pour in the flour mixture and whip with hand mixer until sanity and smooth.
5. Scrape the batter into the cake pan and level the batter with a spatula.
6. Place the cake pan into the zone 1 drawer. Select Bake button and adjust temperature to 165°C, set time to 20 minutes and press Start.
7. Check the doneness during the last 5 minutes of the baking. Until a toothpick inserted in the centre comes out clean, invert the cake on a cooling rack and allow to cool for 15 minutes before slicing to serve.

Broiled Grapefruit

Prep time: 5 minutes | Cook time: 5 minutes | Serves 4

- 2 grapefruit, sliced in half
- 2 tablespoons brown sugar

1. Preheat the grill function of the air fryer.
2. Sprinkle the grapefruit with brown sugar.
3. Place the grapefruit halves in the air fryer basket, cut side up.
4. Broil for 5 minutes, or until the sugar is melted and bubbly.
5. Serve warm.

Spicy Cheese-Stuffed Mushrooms

Prep time: 5 minutes | Cook time: 8 minutes | Serves 20

- 4 ounces cream cheese, softened
- 6 tablespoons shredded cheddar cheese
- 2 tablespoons chopped pickled jalapeños
- 20 medium button mushrooms, stems removed
- 2 tablespoons olive oil
- 1/4 teaspoon salt
- 1/8 teaspoon ground black pepper

1. Preheat the oven to 200°C/400°F.
2. In a large bowl, mix cream cheese, cheddar cheese, and jalapeños together.
3. Drizzle the mushrooms with olive oil, then sprinkle with salt and pepper.
4. Spoon 2 tablespoons of the cheese mixture into each mushroom and place them on a baking tray lined with parchment paper.
5. Bake the stuffed mushrooms in the preheated oven for about 8-10 minutes, checking halfway through cooking to ensure even cooking, and rearranging if necessary. The mushrooms are done when they are golden and the cheese is bubbling.
6. Once done, remove the stuffed mushrooms from the oven and serve them warm.

Coconut And Berries Cream

Prep time: 5 minutes | Cook time: 30 minutes | Serves 6

- 12 ounces blackberries
- 6 ounces raspberries
- 12 ounces blueberries
- 3/4 cup granulated sugar substitute (such as Swerve)
- 4 ounces coconut cream

1. Preheat the oven to 180°C/350°F.
2. In a bowl, mix all the ingredients and whisk well.
3. Divide the mixture into 6 ramekins and place them on a baking tray lined with parchment paper.
4. Bake the ramekins in the preheated oven for 30-35 minutes, until the mixture is set and the top is slightly golden.
5. Once done, remove the ramekins from the oven and let them cool down.
6. Serve the coconut and berries cream chilled or at room temperature.

Cream Cheese Shortbread Cookies

Prep time: 5 minutes | Cook time: 20 minutes | Serves 12

- ¼ cup coconut oil, melted
- 2 ounces cream cheese, softened
- ½ cup granular erythritol
- 1 large egg, whisked
- 2 cups blanched finely ground almond flour
- 1 teaspoon almond extract

1. In a large bowl, cream together the butter, cream cheese, and erythritol until light and fluffy.
2. Beat in the egg, almond flour, and almond extract until the mixture comes together to form a firm ball.
3. Place the dough on a sheet of plastic wrap and roll into a 12-inch long log shape. Wrap the log tightly in the plastic wrap and refrigerate for 30 minutes to chill.
4. Preheat the air fryer to 180°C.
5. Remove the log from the plastic wrap and slice it into 12 equal cookies.
6. Cut two sheets of parchment paper to fit the air fryer basket. Place six cookies on each ungreased sheet of parchment paper.
7. Place one sheet with cookies into the air fryer basket and set the timer for 10 minutes. Flip the cookies halfway through cooking.
8. Once the cookies are lightly golden, remove them from the air fryer and let them cool for 15 minutes before serving to avoid crumbling.
9. Repeat with the remaining cookies.

Cinnamon-Sugar Pretzel Bites

Prep time: 10 minutes | Cook time: 10 minutes | Serves 4

- 120g plain flour
- 1 teaspoon quick-rise yeast
- 2 tablespoons caster sugar, divided
- ¼ teaspoon salt
- 1 tablespoon olive oil
- 80ml warm water
- 2 teaspoons bicarbonate of soda
- 1 teaspoon ground cinnamon
- Cooking spray

1. In a large bowl, mix flour, yeast, 2 teaspoons sugar, and salt until combined.
2. Pour in oil and water and stir until a dough begins to form and pull away from the edges of the bowl. Remove dough from the bowl and transfer to a lightly floured surface. Knead 10 minutes until dough is mostly smooth.
3. Spritz dough with cooking spray and place into a large clean bowl. Cover with plastic wrap and let rise 1 hour.
4. Preheat the air fryer to 200°C (400°F).
5. Press dough into a 15cm × 10cm rectangle. Cut dough into twenty-four even pieces.
6. Fill a medium saucepan over medium-high heat halfway with water and bring to a boil. Add bicarbonate of soda and let it boil 1 minute, then add pretzel bites. You may need to work in batches. Cook 45 seconds, then remove from water and drain. They will be puffy but should have mostly maintained their shape.
7. Spritz pretzel bites with cooking spray. Place in the air fryer basket and cook 5 minutes until golden brown.
8. In a small bowl, mix remaining sugar and cinnamon. When pretzel bites are done cooking, immediately toss in cinnamon and sugar mixture and serve.

Chapter 5
Fish and Seafood Recipes

Crumb-Topped Sole

Prep time: 10 minutes | Cook time: 10 minutes | Serves 4

- 3 tablespoons mayonnaise
- 3 tablespoons grated Parmesan cheese, divided
- 2 teaspoons mustard seed
- ¼ teaspoon pepper
- 4 sole fillets
- 100g soft bread crumbs
- 1 green onion, finely chopped
- ½ teaspoon ground mustard
- 2 teaspoons butter, melted
- Cooking spray

1. Mix mayonnaise, 2 tablespoons cheese, mustard seed and pepper; spread over tops of fillets.
2. Press your chosen zone - "Zone 1" or "Zone 2" and then rotate the knob to select "Air Fry".
3. Set the temperature to 190 degrees C, and then set the time for 5 minutes to preheat.
4. After preheating, spray the Air-Fryer basket of each zone with cooking spray, arrange fish in a single layer, and spritz them with cooking spray.
5. Slide the basket into the Air Fryer and set the time for 5 minutes.
6. Meanwhile, combine bread crumbs, onion, crushed mustard, and the remaining 1 tablespoon of cheese in a small bowl; whisk in butter.
7. Spritz top with cooking spray and spoon over fillets, carefully patting to adhere and cook for 5 more minutes.
8. After cooking time is completed, place them on a serving plate and serve.

Teriyaki Salmon

Prep time: 10 minutes | Cook time: 15 minutes | Serves 3

- 8 tsp Less Sodium Teriyaki
- 3 tsp honey
- 2 cubes of frozen garlic
- 2 tsp extra virgin olive oil
- 3 pieces of wild salmon

1. Whisk everything together to make the marinade.
2. Pour over defrosted fish and marinate for 20 minutes.
3. Press your chosen zone - "Zone 1" or "Zone 2" and then rotate the knob to select "Air Fry".
4. Set the temperature to 175 degrees C, and then set the time for 5 minutes to preheat.
5. After preheating, place a foil sheet on each basket, spray the Air-Fryer basket of each zone with cooking spray, arrange them in a single layer, and spritz them with cooking spray.
6. Slide the basket into the Air Fryer and set the time for 12 minutes.
7. Carefully turn them and cook them 6 minutes longer.
8. After cooking time is completed, place them on a serving plate and serve.

Honey Glazed Salmon

Prep time: 10 minutes | Cook time: 12 minutes | Serves 2

- 2 salmon fillets
- ¾ teaspoon toasted sesame oil
- 1 teaspoon sesame seeds
- ½ tablespoon low-sodium soy sauce
- ½ tablespoon honey
- ¼ teaspoon crushed chili flakes
- Salt and pepper, to taste

1. In a shallow dish, add soy sauce, salt, pepper and oil. Whisk well.
2. Pour the mixture over salmon-fillets and rub all over the fish.
3. Cover the dish and place the mixture in refrigerator for about 15 minutes.
4. Remove the salmon fillets from refrigerator and shake off the excess marinade.
5. Line each basket of "Zone 1" and "Zone 2" of Ninja Foodi 2-Basket Air Fryer with a piece of foil.
6. Press your chosen zone - "Zone 1" or "Zone 2" and then rotate the knob to select "Air Fry".
7. Set the heat to 180 degrees C and then set the time for 5 minutes to preheat.
8. After preheating, arrange salmon fillets into the basket of each zone.
9. Brush with honey and sprinkle with chili flakes and sesame seeds.
10. Slide the basket into the Air Fryer and set the time for 12 minutes.
11. After cooking time is completed, remove the salmon fillets from Air Fryer and serve hot.

Super Crunchy Flounder Fillets

Prep time: 5 minutes | Cook time: 6 minutes | Serves 2

- 75g plain flour or tapioca flour
- 1 large egg white
- 1 tablespoon water
- ¾ teaspoon table salt
- 100g breadcrumbs (gluten-free, if needed)
- 2 113g skinless plaice fillets
- Spray oil

1. Preheat the air fryer to 200°C.
2. Set up three shallow dishes: one for the flour, one for the egg white mixed with water and salt, and one for the breadcrumbs.
3. Dip one fillet in the flour, coating both sides, then dip it into the egg white mixture, letting any excess mixture drip off. Coat it with breadcrumbs, pressing them gently to create an even crust. Repeat with the other fillet.
4. Place the fillets in the air fryer basket, making sure they do not touch. Spray them generously with oil.
5. Air fry for 6 minutes or until golden and crispy.
6. Use a non-stick spatula to transfer the fillets to a wire rack to cool for a minute or two before serving.

Tilapia with Garlic and Lemon
Prep time: 10 minutes | Cook time: 12 minutes | Serves 4

- 4 tilapia fillets
- 1 teaspoon lemon pepper seasoning
- 1 teaspoon garlic powder
- 1 teaspoon onion powder
- Salt and black pepper, to taste

1. Add lemon pepper seasoning, garlic powder, onion powder, salt and black pepper in a shallow dish. Mix well.
2. Coat the tilapia fillets with oil and then rub with spice mixture.
3. Grease basket of Ninja Foodi 2-Basket Air Fryer.
4. Press your chosen zone - "Zone 1" or "Zone 2" and then rotate the knob to select "Air Fry".
5. Set the temperature to 180 degrees C and then set the time for 5 minutes to preheat.
6. After preheating, arrange tilapia fillets into the basket of each zone.
7. Slide the basket into the Air Fryer and set the time for 12 minutes.
8. While cooking, flip the tilapia fillets once halfway through.
9. After cooking time is completed, remove the tilapia fillets and from Air Fryer and serve hot.

Potato Chip-crusted Cod
Prep time: 5 minutes | Cook time: 20 minutes | Serves 2

- 1/2 cup crushed potato crisps
- 1 tsp chopped fresh tarragon
- 1/8 tsp salt
- 1 tsp cayenne pepper
- 1 tbsp Dijon mustard
- 60ml buttermilk
- 1 tsp lemon juice
- 1 tbsp butter, melted
- 2 cod fillets

1. Preheat air fryer to 180°C.
2. In a bowl, mix together the crushed potato crisps, tarragon, salt, and cayenne pepper.
3. In another bowl, mix the Dijon mustard, buttermilk, lemon juice, and melted butter.
4. Dip each cod fillet in the buttermilk mixture and then coat with the potato crisp mixture.
5. Place the cod fillets in the greased frying basket and Air Fry for 10 minutes, or until the fish is cooked through and flakes easily with a fork.
6. Serve immediately.

Lemon Pepper Salmon
Prep time: 10 minutes | Cook time: 10 minutes | Serves 4

- 2 lemons, zested and sliced
- ½ teaspoon salt
- 4 (110g) salmon fillets
- 1 tablespoon avocado oil
- 1 teaspoon fresh black pepper
- 1 teaspoon garlic powder

1. Grease basket of Ninja Foodi 2-Basket Air Fryer.
2. Press your chosen zone - "Zone 1" or "Zone 2" and then rotate the knob to select "Air Fry".
3. Set the heat to 190 degrees C and then set the time for 5 minutes to preheat.
4. Season the salmon fillets with lemon, salt, garlic powder, black pepper and avocado oil.
5. After preheating, arrange 2 salmon fillets into the basket of each zone.
6. Slide the basket into the Air Fryer and set the time for 10 minutes.
7. After cooking time is completed, remove the salmon fillets from Air Fryer and serve hot.

Crispy Catfish
Prep time: 10 minutes | Cook time: 20 minutes | Serves 2

- 455g catfish filets
- 3 drops hot sauce
- 2½ tablespoons plain flour
- ¼ teaspoon black pepper
- 120ml buttermilk
- 80g polenta
- 1 tablespoon Cajun seasoning
- Salt, to taste

1. In a shallow dish, add hot sauce, plain flour, black pepper, buttermilk, polenta, Cajun seasoning and salt. Mix well.
2. Add the catfish fillets and coat evenly with the mixture.
3. Grease basket of Ninja Foodi 2-Basket Air Fryer.
4. Press your chosen zone - "Zone 1" or "Zone 2" and then rotate the knob to select "Air Fry".
5. Set the temperature to 200 degrees C and then set the time for 5 minutes to preheat.
6. After preheating, arrange catfish fillets into the basket of each zone.
7. Slide the basket into the Air Fryer and set the time for 20 minutes.
8. While cooking, flip the fish fillets once halfway through.
9. After cooking time is completed, remove the fish fillets from Air Fryer and serve hot.

Spicy Cod Fillets

Prep time: 15 minutes | Cook time: 16 minutes | Serves 6

- 6 cod fillets
- 3 tablespoons almond flour
- 1 teaspoon smoked paprika
- 30g gluten-free flour
- 2 teaspoons Cajun seasoning
- ½ teaspoon garlic powder
- Salt and pepper, to taste

1. Add almond flour, smoked paprika, gluten-free flour, Cajun seasoning, garlic powder, salt and pepper in a shallow dish. Whisk well.
2. Coat the fillets with flour mixture and refrigerate for about 2 hours.
3. Grease basket of Ninja Foodi 2-Basket Air Fryer.
4. Press your chosen zone - "Zone 1" or "Zone 2" and then rotate the knob to select "Air Fry".
5. Set the temperature to 200 degrees C and then set the time for 5 minutes to preheat.
6. After preheating, arrange the cod fillets into the basket of each zone.
7. Slide the basket into the Air Fryer and set the time for 16 minutes.
8. While cooking, flip the cod fillets once halfway through.
9. After cooking time is completed, remove the cod fillets from Air Fryer and serve hot.

Garlicky Sea Bass With Root Veggies

Prep time: 5 minutes | Cook time: 25 minutes | Serves 4

- 1 carrot, diced
- 1 parsnip, diced
- ½ swede, diced
- ½ turnip, diced
- 60 ml olive oil
- Celery salt to taste
- 4 sea bass fillets
- ½ tsp onion powder
- 2 garlic cloves, minced
- 1 lemon, sliced

1. Preheat the air fryer to 380°F (190°C).
2. In a small bowl, toss the diced carrot, parsnip, swede, and turnip with olive oil and celery salt.
3. Season the sea bass fillets with onion powder and place them in the air fryer basket. Spread the minced garlic over the top of the fillets and cover with lemon slices.
4. Add the prepared vegetables to the basket around and on top of the fish.
5. Air fry for 15 minutes.
6. Serve and enjoy!

Basil Crab Cakes With Fresh Salad

Prep time: 10 minutes | Cook time: 25 minutes | Serves 2

- 8 oz white crab meat
- 2 tbsp mayonnaise
- ½ tsp Dijon mustard
- ½ tsp lemon juice
- ½ tsp lemon zest
- 2 tsp minced white onion
- ¼ tsp prepared horseradish
- ¼ cup plain flour
- 1 egg white, beaten
- 1 tbsp fresh basil, finely chopped
- 1 tbsp olive oil
- 2 tsp white wine vinegar
- Salt and pepper to taste
- 4 oz rocket (arugula)
- ½ cup blackberries
- ¼ cup pine nuts
- 2 lemon wedges

1. Preheat air fryer to 400°F (200°C).
2. In a mixing bowl, combine the white crab meat, mayonnaise, mustard, lemon juice and zest, white onion, horseradish, plain flour, egg white, and fresh basil.
3. Shape the mixture into 4 patties.
4. Place the patties in the lightly greased frying basket and air fry for 10 minutes, flipping once halfway through cooking.
5. In a separate bowl, whisk together the olive oil, white wine vinegar, salt, and pepper to create the dressing.
6. Toss the rocket (arugula) in the dressing, then divide between two medium-sized bowls.
7. Place 2 crab cakes on top of each salad and scatter with blackberries, pine nuts, and lemon wedges.
8. Serve warm.

Horseradish-Crusted Salmon Fillets

Prep time: 5 minutes | Cook time: 8 minutes | Serves 3

- 75g fresh breadcrumbs
- 60g unsalted butter, melted and cooled
- 60ml jarred prepared white horseradish
- Cooking spray
- 4 170g skin-on salmon fillets

1. Preheat the air fryer to 200°C/180°C fan/gas mark 6.
2. Mix the breadcrumbs, butter, and horseradish in a bowl until well combined.
3. Take the basket out of the air fryer. Generously spray the skin side of each fillet. Pick them up one by one with a non-stick safe spatula and set them in the basket skin side down with as much air space between them as possible. Divide the breadcrumb mixture between the fillets, coating the top of each fillet with an even layer. Generously coat the breadcrumb mixture with cooking spray.
4. Return the basket to the air fryer and air-fry undisturbed for 8 minutes, or until the topping has lightly browned and the fish is firm but not hard.
5. Use a non-stick safe spatula to transfer the salmon fillets to serving plates. Cool for 5 minutes before serving. Because of the butter in the topping, it will stay very hot for quite a while. Take care, especially if you're serving these fillets to children.

Bacon-Wrapped Cajun Scallops

Prep time: 5 minutes | Cook time: 13 minutes | Serves 4

- 8 rashers of streaky bacon
- 8 scallops, rinsed and patted dry
- 1 teaspoon Cajun seasoning
- 4 tablespoons salted butter, melted

1. Preheat the air fryer to 190°C.
2. Place the bacon in the air fryer basket and cook for 3 minutes. Remove the bacon and wrap each scallop in one slice of bacon, securing it with a toothpick.
3. Sprinkle the Cajun seasoning evenly over the scallops. Lightly spray the scallops with cooking spray and place them in the air fryer basket in a single layer. Cook for 10 minutes, turning halfway through cooking time, until the scallops are opaque and firm and the internal temperature reaches at least 54°C. Drizzle with melted butter. Serve warm.

Butternut Squash Wrapped Halibut Fillets

Prep time: 5 minutes | Cook time: 11 minutes | Serves 3

- 15 long spiralized, peeled and seeded strands of butternut squash
- 3 skinless halibut fillets, each weighing 140-170g
- 3 tablespoons melted butter
- 3/4 teaspoon mild paprika
- 3/4 teaspoon table salt
- 3/4 teaspoon ground black pepper

1. Preheat the air fryer to 190°C.
2. Take 5 long strands of butternut squash and wrap them around a fillet. Repeat with the remaining fillets and squash strands.
3. In a small bowl, mix the melted butter, paprika, salt, and pepper. Brush this mixture over the squash-wrapped fillets on all sides.
4. When the air fryer reaches the desired temperature, place the fillets in the basket with as much air space between them as possible. Air-fry undisturbed for 10 minutes or until the squash strands have browned but not burned. If the air fryer temperature is set at 180°C, you may need to add 1 minute to the cooking time. In any event, watch the fish carefully after the 8-minute mark.
5. Use a nonstick-safe spatula to gently transfer the fillets to a serving platter or plates. Cool for only a minute or so before serving.

Prawn Skewers

Prep time: 5 minutes | Cook time: 5 minutes | Serves 5

- 1 tablespoon olive oil
- 2 tablespoons tamari soy sauce
- 2 tablespoons honey
- 2 tablespoons Korean Gochujang
- 1 tablespoon lemon juice
- 1 teaspoon minced garlic
- 900g peeled and cleaned prawns

1. Before usage, soak bamboo skewers in water for 30 minutes.
2. Combine olive oil, soy sauce, honey, Korean Gochujang, lemon juice, and garlic in a mixing bowl.
3. Toss the prawns into the bowl and toss to coat.
4. Marinate for about 30 minutes. Thread about 5 prawns to each skewer.
5. Press your chosen zone - "Zone 1" or "Zone 2" and then rotate the knob to select "Air Fry".
6. Set the temperature to 175 degrees C, and then set the time for 5 minutes to preheat.
7. After preheating, spray the Air-Fryer basket of each zone with cooking spray, arrange them in a single layer, and spritz them with cooking spray.
8. Slide the basket into the Air Fryer and set the time for 3 minutes.
9. Carefully turn them and cook them 2 minutes longer.
10. After cooking time is completed, place them on a serving plate and serve.

Lemon-Dill Salmon With Green Beans

Prep time: 5 minutes | Cook time: 20 minutes | Serves 4

- 20 halved cherry tomatoes
- 4 tbsp butter
- 4 garlic cloves, minced
- ¼ cup chopped dill
- Salt and pepper to taste
- 4 wild-caught salmon fillets
- ¼ cup white wine
- 1 lemon, thinly sliced
- 1 lb green beans, trimmed
- 2 tbsp chopped parsley

1. Preheat air fryer to 200°C / 390°F.
2. Combine butter, garlic, dill, wine, salt, and pepper in a small bowl.
3. Spread the seasoned butter over the top of the salmon.
4. Arrange the fish in a single layer in the frying basket.
5. Top with ½ of the lemon slices and surround the fish with green beans and tomatoes.
6. Bake for 12-15 minutes until salmon is cooked and vegetables are tender.
7. Top with parsley and serve with lemon slices on the side.

Garlic-Lemon Steamer Clams

Prep time: 5 minutes | Cook time 30minutes |Serves 2

- 25 British clams, scrubbed
- 2 tbsp butter, melted
- 1 garlic clove, minced
- 2 lemon wedges

1. Add the clams to a large bowl filled with water and let sit for 10 minutes. Drain. Pour more water and let sit for 10 more minutes. Drain.
2. Preheat the air fryer to 350°F (180°C).
3. Place the clams in the air fryer basket and air fry for 7 minutes. Discard any clams that don´t open.
4. Remove the clams from the shells and place them into a large serving dish.
5. Drizzle with melted butter and garlic and squeeze lemon on top.
6. Serve immediately.

Simple Sesame Squid On The Grill

Prep time: 5 minutes | Cook time:10minutes |Serves 3

- 680 grams squid, cleaned
- 2 tablespoons toasted sesame oil
- Salt and pepper to taste

1. Preheat the air fryer to 200°C/400°F.
2. Place the grill pan accessory in the air fryer.
3. Season the squid with sesame oil, salt, and pepper.
4. Grill the squid for 10 minutes, flipping halfway through cooking time, until cooked through and lightly charred.
5. Serve immediately with your preferred sides.

Chinese Firecracker Shrimp

Prep time: 5 minutes | Cook time: 20 minutes | Serves 4

- 500g peeled prawns, deveined
- 2 spring onions, chopped
- 2 tbsp sesame seeds
- Salt and pepper to taste
- 1 egg
- 120g plain flour
- 75g panko breadcrumbs
- 80ml sour cream
- 2 tbsp Sriracha sauce
- 60ml sweet chili sauce

1. Preheat air fryer to 200°C (400°F).
2. Set out three small bowls.
3. In the first, add flour. In the second, beat the egg. In the third, add the crumbs.
4. Season the prawns with salt and pepper.
5. Dip the prawns in the flour, then dredge in the egg, and finally in the breadcrumbs. Place the prawns in the greased frying basket and Air Fry for 8 minutes, flipping once until crispy.
6. Combine sour cream, Sriracha, and sweet chili sauce in a bowl.
7. Top the prawns with sesame seeds and spring onions and serve with the chili sauce.

Seared Scallops In Beurre Blanc

Prep time: 5 minutes | Cook time: 15 minutes | Serves 4

- 450g sea scallops
- Salt and pepper to taste
- 2 tbsp unsalted butter, melted
- 1 lemon, zested and juiced
- 2 tbsp dry white wine

1. Preheat the air fryer to 200°C/400°F.
2. Season the scallops with salt and pepper to taste, then place them in a bowl.
3. In another bowl, combine the melted unsalted butter, lemon zest, lemon juice, and white wine. Mix well.
4. Place the scallops in a baking pan and drizzle the butter mixture over them.
5. Air fry for 8-11 minutes, flipping the scallops over after about 5 minutes, until they are opaque.
6. Serve immediately and enjoy!

Breaded Tilapia

Prep time: 10 minutes | Cook time: 12 minutes | Serves 6

- 4 large eggs
- ½ teaspoon cayenne pepper powder
- 4 large tilapia fillets, patted dry
- 6 tablespoons plain flour
- 300g breadcrumbs
- Salt and pepper, to taste

1. In a shallow dish, beat eggs and add cayenne pepper, plain flour, salt and pepper in it. Mix well.
2. Add breadcrumbs in another bowl and set aside.
3. Dip the tilapia fillets into egg mixture and then coat with the breadcrumbs mixture.
4. Grease basket of Ninja Foodi 2-Basket Air Fryer.
5. Press your chosen zone - "Zone 1" or "Zone 2" and then rotate the knob to select "Air Fry".
6. Set the heat to 180 degrees C and then set the time for 5 minutes to preheat.
7. After preheating, arrange tilapia fillets into the basket of each zone.
8. Slide the basket into the Air Fryer and set the time for 12 minutes.
9. While cooking, flip the tilapia fillets once halfway through.
10. After cooking time is completed, remove the tilapia fillets and from Air Fryer and serve hot.

Nacho Chips Crusted Prawns
Prep time: 5 minutes | Cook time: 8 minutes | Serves 2

- 340g prawns, peeled and deveined
- 1 large egg
- 142g Nacho flavored chips, finely crushed

1. In a shallow bowl, beat the egg.
2. In another bowl, place the nacho chips
3. Dip each prawn into the beaten egg and then, coat with the crushed nacho chips.
4. Set the temperature of air fryer to 180°C. Grease an air fryer basket.
5. Arrange prawns into the prepared air fryer basket.
6. Air fry for about 8 minutes.
7. Remove from air fryer and transfer the prawns onto serving plates.
8. Serve hot.

Pecan-Crusted Tilapia
Prep time: 5 minutes | Cook time: 8 minutes | Serves 4

- 450g skinless, boneless tilapia fillets
- 60g butter, melted
- 1 teaspoon minced fresh or dried rosemary
- 100g finely chopped pecans
- 1 teaspoon sea salt
- ¼ teaspoon paprika
- 2 tablespoons chopped parsley
- 1 lemon, cut into wedges

1. Pat the tilapia fillets dry with paper towels.
2. Pour the melted butter over the fillets and flip the fillets to coat them completely.
3. In a medium bowl, mix together the rosemary, pecans, salt, and paprika.
4. Preheat the air fryer to 180°C/350°F.
5. Place the tilapia fillets into the air fryer basket and top with the pecan coating. Cook for 6 to 8 minutes. The fish should be firm to the touch and flake easily when fully cooked.
6. Remove the fish from the air fryer. Top the fish with chopped parsley and serve with lemon wedges.

Lemon-Roasted Salmon Fillets
Prep time: 5 minutes | Cook time: 7 minutes | Serves 3

- 3 6-ounce skin-on salmon fillets
- Olive oil spray
- 9 very thin lemon slices
- ¾ teaspoon ground black pepper
- ¼ teaspoon table salt

1. Preheat the air fryer to 200°C (400°F).
2. Generously coat the skin of each of the fillets with olive oil spray. Set the fillets skin side down on your work surface. Place three overlapping lemon slices down the length of each salmon fillet. Sprinkle them with the pepper and salt. Coat lightly with olive oil spray.
3. Use a nonstick-safe spatula to transfer the fillets one by one to the basket, leaving as much air space between them as possible. Air-fry undisturbed for 7 minutes, or until cooked through.
4. Use a nonstick-safe spatula to transfer the fillets to serving plates. Cool for only a minute or two before serving.

Crunchy Flounder Gratin
Prep time: 10 minutes | Cook time: 20 minutes | Serves 4

- 25g grated Parmesan
- 4 flounder fillets
- 60g butter, melted
- 25g panko bread crumbs
- ½ tsp paprika
- 1 egg
- Salt and pepper to taste
- ½ tsp dried oregano
- ½ tsp dried basil
- 1 tsp dried thyme
- 1 lemon, quartered
- 1 tbsp chopped parsley

1. Preheat air fryer to 190°C.
2. In a bowl, whisk together egg until smooth.
3. Brush the fillets on both sides with some of the butter.
4. Combine the rest of the butter, bread crumbs, Parmesan cheese, salt, paprika, thyme, oregano, basil, and pepper in a small bowl until crumbly.
5. Dip the fish into the egg and then into the bread crumb mixture and coat completely.
6. Transfer the fish to the frying basket and bake for 5 minutes.
7. Carefully flip the fillets and bake for another 6 minutes until crispy and golden on the outside.
8. Garnish with lemon wedges and parsley.
9. Serve and enjoy.

Chapter 6
Poultry Mains Recipes

Fajita Stuffed Chicken

Prep time: 10 minutes | Cook time: 15 minutes | Serves 2

- 2 boneless skinless chicken breast halves
- ½ onion, thinly sliced
- ½ teaspoon ground cumin
- ½ teaspoon chili powder
- ½ tablespoon olive oil
- ¼ medium green pepper, thinly sliced
- ¼ teaspoon salt
- ⅛ teaspoon garlic powder
- 50g cheddar cheese, cut into slices

1. Cut each chicken breast in the thickest part and fill with green peppers and onion.
2. In a small bowl, combine olive oil and seasonings.
3. Rub over chicken.
4. Grease basket of Ninja Foodi 2-Basket Air Fryer.
5. Press your chosen zone - "Zone 1" or "Zone 2" and then rotate the knob to select "Air Fry".
6. Set the heat to 190 degrees C and then set the time for 5 minutes to preheat.
7. After preheating, arrange chicken breasts into the basket of each zone.
8. Slide the basket into the Air Fryer and set the time for 15 minutes.
9. After cooking time is completed, remove the chicken breasts from Air Fryer and serve hot.

Almond Chicken

Prep time: 15 minutes | Cook time: 30 minutes | Serves 2

- 2 chicken breast halves, boneless and skinless
- 2 small eggs
- 1 teaspoon garlic salt
- 4 tablespoons buttermilk
- 70g silvered almonds, finely chopped
- ½ teaspoon pepper

1. Take a shallow bowl, whisk egg, buttermilk, pepper and garlic salt.
2. Place almonds in another shallow bowl.
3. Dip chicken breasts into the egg mixture and then coat with almonds.
4. Grease basket of Ninja Foodi 2-Basket Air Fryer.
5. Press your chosen zone - "Zone 1" or "Zone 2" and then rotate the knob to select "Air Fry".
6. Set the temperature to 175 degrees C and then set the time for 5 minutes to preheat.
7. After preheating, arrange the chicken into the basket of each zone.
8. Slide the basket into the Air Fryer and set the time for 15 to 18 minutes.
9. After cooking time is completed, remove chicken from Air Fryer and serve hot.

Gingered Chicken Drumsticks
Prep time: 10 minutes | **Cook time:** 25 minutes | **Serves 6**

- 120ml full-fat coconut milk
- 4 teaspoons fresh ginger, minced
- 4 teaspoons galangal, minced
- 2 teaspoons ground turmeric
- Salt, as required
- 6 (150g) chicken drumsticks

1. In a large bowl, place the coconut milk, galangal, ginger, and spices and mix well.
2. Add the chicken drumsticks and coat with the marinade generously.
3. Refrigerate to marinate for at least 6-8 hours.
4. Grease basket of Ninja Foodi 2-Basket Air Fryer.
5. Press your chosen zone - "Zone 1" or "Zone 2" and then rotate the knob to select "Air Fry".
6. Set the temperature to 190 degrees C and then set the time for 5 minutes to preheat.
7. After preheating, arrange 3 drumsticks into the basket of each zone.
8. Slide the basket into the Air Fryer and set the time for 25 minutes.
9. After cooking time is completed, remove the drumsticks from Air Fryer and serve hot.

Southern Style Chicken
Prep time: 10 minutes | **Cook time:** 20 minutes | **Serves 6**

- 900g chicken, cut up
- 85g crushed Ritz crackers
- ½ teaspoon paprika
- ½ teaspoon garlic salt
- ½ tablespoon minced fresh parsley
- ⅛ teaspoon rubbed sage
- ⅛ teaspoon ground cumin
- ¼ teaspoon pepper
- 1 small egg, beaten

1. Take a bowl, add all ingredients except chicken and egg. Mix well.
2. Take another bowl and whisk egg.
3. Dip chicken in egg, then coat with cracker mixture.
4. Grease basket of Ninja Foodi 2-Basket Air Fryer.
5. Press your chosen zone - "Zone 1" or "Zone 2" and then rotate the knob to select "Air Fry".
6. Set the heat to 190 degrees C and then set the time for 5 minutes to preheat.
7. After preheating, arrange chicken into the basket of each zone.
8. Slide the basket into the Air Fryer and set the time for 15 to 20 minutes.
9. After cooking time is completed, remove the chicken from Air Fryer and place onto a platter.
10. Serve and enjoy.

Garlicky Duck Legs
Prep time: 10 minutes | **Cook time:** 30 minutes | **Serves 4**

- 4 garlic cloves, minced
- 2 tablespoons fresh parsley, chopped
- 2 teaspoons five-spice powder
- Salt and ground black pepper, as required
- 4 duck legs

1. In a bowl, add the garlic, parsley, five-spice powder, salt and black pepper and mix until well combined.
2. Rub the duck legs with garlic mixture generously.
3. Grease basket of Ninja Foodi 2-Basket Air Fryer.
4. Press your chosen zone - "Zone 1" or "Zone 2" and then rotate the knob to select "Air Fry".
5. Set the temperature to 170 degrees C and then set the time for 5 minutes to preheat.
6. After preheating, arrange 2 duck legs into the basket of each zone.
7. Slide the basket into the Air Fryer and set the time for 30 minutes.
8. After cooking time is completed, remove the duck legs from Air Fryer and serve hot.

Yummy Stuffed Chicken Breast
Prep time: 5 minutes | **Cook time:** 15 minutes | **Serves 4**

- 2 chicken fillets, skinless and boneless, each cut into 2 pieces
- 4 Brie cheese slices
- 1 tablespoon chives, finely chopped
- 4 cured ham slices
- Salt and black pepper, to taste

1. Preheat the Air fryer to 180°C/355°F and grease an Air fryer basket.
2. Make a horizontal slit in each chicken piece and season with salt and black pepper.
3. Insert a cheese slice into each slit and sprinkle with chives.
4. Wrap each chicken piece with a slice of ham and transfer into the Air fryer basket.
5. Cook for about 15 minutes or until the chicken is fully cooked, flipping halfway through.
6. Dish out and serve hot.

Tuscan Stuffed Chicken

Prep time: 5 minutes | Cook time: 30 minutes | Serves 4

- 85g ricotta cheese
- 225g Tuscan kale, chopped
- 4 chicken breasts
- 1 tbsp chicken seasoning
- Salt and pepper to taste
- 1 tsp paprika

1. Preheat air fryer to 190°C. Soften the ricotta cheese in a microwave-safe bowl for 15 seconds. Combine in a bowl along with Tuscan kale. Set aside. Cut 4-5 slits in the top of each chicken breast about ¾ of the way down. Season with chicken seasoning, salt, and pepper.
2. Place the chicken with the slits facing up in the greased frying basket. Lightly spray the chicken with oil. Bake for 6-8 minutes. Slide-out and stuff the cream cheese mixture into the chicken slits. Sprinkle ½ tsp of paprika and cook for another 3 minutes. Serve and enjoy!

Family Chicken Fingers

Prep time: 5 minutes | Cook time: 30 minutes | Serves 4

- 450g chicken breast strips
- 1 tbsp chicken seasoning
- ½ tsp mustard powder
- Salt and pepper to taste
- 2 eggs
- 100g breadcrumbs

1. Preheat air fryer to 200°C. Add the chicken strips to a large bowl along with chicken seasoning, mustard, salt, and pepper; mix well.
2. Set up two small bowls. In one bowl, beat the eggs. In the second bowl, add the breadcrumbs. Dip the chicken in the egg, then coat it in breadcrumbs.
3. Place the chicken strips in the air fryer basket. Lightly spray with cooking oil, then Air Fry for 8 minutes, shaking the basket once until crispy and cooked through. Serve warm.

Chicken Tenders With Basil-strawberry Glaze

Prep time: 5 minutes | Cook time: 20 minutes | Serves 4

- 450g chicken tenders
- 60ml strawberry jam
- 3 tbsp chopped fresh basil
- 1 tsp orange juice
- ½ tsp orange zest
- Salt and pepper, to taste

1. In a bowl, mix together the strawberry jam, chopped basil, orange juice, orange zest, salt, and pepper.
2. Add the chicken tenders to the bowl and stir to coat evenly. Cover and marinate in the fridge for 30 minutes.
3. Preheat the air fryer to 180°C.
4. Place the marinated chicken tenders in the air fryer basket and cook for 4-6 minutes.
5. Gently shake the basket and turn over the chicken tenders. Cook for an additional 5 minutes, or until the chicken is cooked through and the coating is crispy and golden brown.
6. Serve the chicken tenders hot, topped with the remaining chopped basil.

Spinach And Feta Stuffed Chicken Breasts
Prep time: 5 minutes | Cook time: 27minutes | Serves 4

- 1 package frozen spinach, thawed and drained well
- 1 cup feta cheese, crumbled
- ½ teaspoon freshly ground black pepper
- 4 boneless chicken breasts
- salt and freshly ground black pepper
- 1 tablespoon olive oil

1. Prepare the filling. Squeeze out as much liquid as possible from the thawed spinach. Roughly chop the spinach and transfer it to a mixing bowl with the feta cheese and the freshly ground black pepper.
2. Prepare the chicken breast. Place the chicken breast on a cutting board and press down on the chicken breast with one hand to keep it stabilised. Make an incision about 2.5cm long in the thickest side of the breast. Move the knife up and down inside the chicken breast, without poking through either the top or the bottom, or the other side of the breast. The inside pocket should be about 7.5cm long, but the opening should only be about 2.5cm wide. If this is too difficult, you can make the incision longer, but you will have to be more careful when cooking the chicken breast since this will expose more of the stuffing.
3. Once you have prepared the chicken breasts, use your fingers to stuff the filling into each pocket, spreading the mixture down as far as you can.
4. Preheat the air fryer to 190°C.
5. Lightly brush or spray the air fryer basket and the chicken breasts with olive oil. Transfer two of the stuffed chicken breasts to the air fryer. Air-fry for 12 minutes, turning the chicken breasts over halfway through the cooking time. Remove the chicken to a resting plate and air-fry the second two breasts for 12 minutes. Return the first batch of chicken to the air fryer with the second batch and air-fry for 3 more minutes. When the chicken is cooked, an instant read thermometer should register 74°C in the thickest part of the chicken, as well as in the stuffing.
6. Remove the chicken breasts and let them rest on a cutting board for 2 to 3 minutes. Slice the chicken on the bias and serve with the slices fanned out.

Teriyaki Chicken Legs
Prep time: 5 minutes | Cook time: 20minutes | Serves 2

- 4 chicken legs
- 4 tablespoons teriyaki sauce
- 1 tablespoon orange juice
- 1 teaspoon smoked paprika
- Cooking spray

1. Preheat the air fryer to 180°C/350°F.
2. Mix together the teriyaki sauce, orange juice, and smoked paprika in a small bowl.
3. Brush the sauce mixture on all sides of the chicken legs.
4. Spray the air fryer basket with cooking spray and place the chicken legs in the basket.
5. Air fry at 180°C/350°F for 6 minutes. Turn the chicken legs over and baste them with the sauce.
6. Air fry for an additional 6 minutes, then turn and baste again.
7. Air fry for another 8 minutes, or until the juices run clear when the chicken is pierced with a fork.
8. Serve hot and enjoy!

Stuffed Chicken Breasts
Prep time: 15 minutes | Cook time: 30 minutes | Serves 4

- 2 tablespoon olive oil
- 85g fresh spinach
- 125g ricotta cheese, shredded
- 4 (100g) skinless, boneless chicken breasts
- Salt and ground black pepper, as required
- 4 tablespoons Parmesan cheese, grated
- ½ teaspoon paprika

1. In a medium frying pan, heat the oil over medium heat and cook the spinach for about 3-4 minutes.
2. Stir in the ricotta and cook for about 40-60 seconds.
3. Remove the frying pan from heat and set aside to cool.
4. Cut slits into the chicken breasts about ½ cm apart but not all the way through.
5. Stuff each chicken breast with the spinach mixture.
6. Season each chicken breast with salt and black pepper and then sprinkle the top with Parmesan cheese and paprika.
7. Grease basket of Ninja Foodi 2-Basket Air Fryer.
8. Press your chosen zone - "Zone 1" or "Zone 2" and then rotate the knob to select "Air Fry".
9. Set the temperature to 200 degrees C and then set the time for 5 minutes to preheat.
10. After preheating, arrange 2 chicken breasts into the basket of each zone.
11. Slide the basket into the Air Fryer and set the time for 25 minutes.
12. After cooking time is completed, remove the chicken breasts from Air Fryer and serve hot.

Rosemary Turkey Legs
Prep time: 10 minutes | Cook time: 30 minutes | Serves 4

- 4 garlic cloves, minced
- 2 tablespoons fresh rosemary, minced
- 2 teaspoons fresh lime zest, finely grated
- 4 tablespoons olive oil
- 2 tablespoons fresh lime juice
- Salt and ground black pepper, as required
- 4 turkey legs

1. In a large baking dish, mix together the garlic, rosemary, lime zest, oil, lime juice, salt, and black pepper.
2. Add the turkey legs and generously coat with marinade.
3. Refrigerate to marinate for about 6-8 hours.
4. Grease basket of Ninja Foodi 2-Basket Air Fryer.
5. Press your chosen zone - "Zone 1" or "Zone 2" and then rotate the knob to select "Air Fry".
6. Set the temperature to 175 degrees C and then set the time for 5 minutes to preheat.
7. After preheating, arrange 2 turkey legs into the basket of each zone.
8. Slide the basket into the Air Fryer and set the time for 30 minutes.
9. While cooking, flip the turkey legs once halfway through.
10. After cooking time is completed, remove the turkey legs from Air Fryer and serve hot.

Peppery Lemon-chicken Breast
Prep time: 5 minutes | Cook time: 20 minutes | Serves 1

- 1 chicken breast
- 1 teaspoon minced garlic
- 2 lemons, rinds and juice reserved
- Salt and pepper to taste

1. Preheat the air fryer to 200°C (400°F).
2. Place the chicken breast in a baking dish that will fit in the air fryer.
3. In a small bowl, combine minced garlic, lemon zest, salt, and pepper. Rub the mixture over the chicken breast.
4. Drizzle the lemon juice over the chicken.
5. Place the baking dish in the air fryer basket.
6. Cook for 20 minutes at 200°C (400°F) or until the chicken is cooked through.
7. Serve hot.

Mushroom & Turkey Bread Pizza
Prep time: 15 minutes | Cook time: 35 minutes | Serves 4

- 10 cooked turkey sausages, sliced
- 1 cup grated mozzarella cheese
- 1 cup grated Cheddar cheese
- 1 French loaf bread
- 2 tbsp butter, softened
- 1 tsp garlic powder
- 1 1/3 cups marinara sauce
- 1 tsp Italian seasoning
- 2 spring onions, chopped
- 1 cup mushrooms, sliced

1. Preheat the air fryer to 190°C.
2. Cut the bread in half crosswise, then split each half horizontally.
3. Combine butter and garlic powder, then spread on the cut sides of the bread.
4. Bake the halves in the fryer for 3-5 minutes or until the leaves start to brown.
5. Set the toasted bread on a work surface and spread marinara sauce over the top.
6. Sprinkle the Italian seasoning, then top with sausages, spring onions, mushrooms, and cheeses.
7. Set the pizzas in the air fryer and Bake for 8-12 minutes or until the cheese is melted and starting to brown.
8. Serve hot.

Lemon Pepper Chicken Wings

Prep time: 5 minutes | Cook time: 16 minutes | Serves 4

- 450g chicken wings
- 1 tsp lemon pepper
- 1 tbsp olive oil
- 1 tsp salt

1. Place the chicken wings in a large mixing bowl.
2. Add the lemon pepper, olive oil, and salt to the bowl and toss well to coat the wings.
3. Preheat the air fryer to 200°C (400°F).
4. Place the chicken wings in the air fryer basket and cook for 8 minutes.
5. Turn the chicken wings over and cook for an additional 8 minutes.
6. Serve and enjoy.

Mumbai Chicken Nuggets

Prep time: 5 minutes | Cook time: 30 minutes | Serves 4

- 450g boneless, skinless chicken breasts
- 4 tsp curry powder
- Salt and pepper to taste
- 1 egg, beaten
- 2 tbsp sesame oil
- 100g panko bread crumbs
- 120g coconut yogurt
- 80g mango chutney
- 60g mayonnaise

1. Preheat the air fryer to 200°C (400°F).
2. Cut the chicken into 2.5cm pieces and sprinkle with 3 tsp of curry powder, salt, and pepper; toss to coat.
3. Beat together the egg and sesame oil in a shallow bowl and scatter the panko onto a separate plate.
4. Dip the chicken in the egg, then in the panko, and press to coat.
5. Lay the coated nuggets on a wire rack as you work.
6. Set the nuggets in the greased frying basket and Air Fry for 7-10 minutes, rearranging once halfway through cooking.
7. While the nuggets are cooking, combine the yogurt, chutney, mayonnaise, and the remaining teaspoon of curry powder in a small bowl.
8. Serve the nuggets with the dipping sauce.

Southern-fried Chicken Livers

Prep time: 5 minutes | Cook time: 12 minutes | Serves 4

- 2 eggs
- 2 tablespoons water
- 75g plain flour
- 150g panko breadcrumbs
- 50g dried breadcrumbs
- 1 teaspoon salt
- ½ teaspoon black pepper
- 570g chicken livers, seasoned with salt to taste
- Oil for misting or cooking spray

1. Beat together the eggs and water in a shallow dish. Place the plain flour in a separate shallow dish.
2. In the bowl of a food processor, combine the panko, dried breadcrumbs, salt, and black pepper. Process until well mixed and panko crumbs are finely crushed. Place the crumbs in a third shallow dish.
3. Dip the chicken livers in the flour, then in the egg wash, and then roll in the panko mixture to coat well with the crumbs.
4. Spray both sides of the livers with oil or cooking spray. In two batches, place the livers in the air fryer basket in a single layer.
5. Cook at 200°C (390°F) for 7 minutes. Spray the livers, turn them over, and spray again. Cook for 5 more minutes, until cooked through and the coating is golden brown.
6. Repeat to cook the remaining livers.

Chicken Burgers With Blue Cheese Sauce

Prep time: 5 minutes | Cook time: 40 minutes | Serves 4

- 60g crumbled blue cheese
- 60g sour cream
- 2 tbsp mayonnaise
- 1 tbsp hot sauce
- Salt to taste
- 3 tbsp buffalo wing sauce
- 450g ground chicken
- 2 tbsp grated carrot
- 2 tbsp diced celery
- 1 egg white
- 4 burger buns

1. In a bowl, whisk together the blue cheese, sour cream, mayonnaise, hot sauce, salt, and 1 tbsp of buffalo sauce. Cover and refrigerate until ready to use.
2. Preheat the air fryer to 180°C. In another bowl, combine the ground chicken, grated carrot, diced celery, egg white, and remaining buffalo sauce. Form the mixture into 4 patties, making a slight indentation in the middle of each.
3. Place the patties in the air fryer basket and cook for 13 minutes until cooked through, flipping once.
4. Toast the burger buns, then assemble the burgers by placing the cooked chicken patties on the bottom half of each bun, then topping with a generous spoonful of the blue cheese sauce. Serve immediately.

Turkey Tenderloin With A Lemon Touch

Prep time: 5 minutes | Cook time: 45 minutes | Serves 4

- 1 lb boneless, skinless turkey breast tenderloin
- Salt and pepper to taste
- ½ tsp garlic powder
- ½ tsp chili powder
- ½ tsp dried thyme
- 1 lemon, juiced
- 1 tbsp chopped coriander

1. Preheat the air fryer to 350°F / 180°C.
2. Pat the turkey dry with a paper towel and season with salt, pepper, garlic powder, chili powder, and thyme.
3. Place the turkey in the frying basket.
4. Squeeze the lemon juice over the turkey and air fry for 10 minutes.
5. Turn the turkey and air fry for another 10-15 minutes, or until cooked through.
6. Allow the turkey to rest for 10 minutes before slicing.
7. Serve sprinkled with coriander and enjoy.

Chicken Cordon Bleu

Prep time: 5 minutes | Cook time: 16 minutes | Serves 2

- 2 boneless, skinless chicken breasts
- ¼ teaspoon salt
- 2 teaspoons Dijon mustard
- 2 ounces deli ham
- 2 ounces Swiss, fontina, or Gruyère cheese
- 40g plain flour
- 1 egg
- 50g breadcrumbs

1. Pat the chicken breasts with a paper towel. Season the chicken with the salt. Pound the chicken breasts to 1½ inches thick. Create a pouch by slicing the side of each chicken breast. Spread 1 teaspoon Dijon mustard inside the pouch of each chicken breast. Wrap a 1-ounce slice of ham around a 1-ounce slice of cheese and place into the pouch. Repeat with the remaining ham and cheese.
2. In a medium bowl, place the flour.
3. In a second bowl, whisk the egg.
4. In a third bowl, place the breadcrumbs.
5. Dredge the chicken in the flour and shake off the excess. Next, dip the chicken into the egg and then in the breadcrumbs. Set the chicken on a plate and repeat with the remaining chicken piece.
6. Preheat the air fryer to 180°C.
7. Place the chicken in the air fryer basket and spray liberally with cooking spray. Cook for 8 minutes, turn the chicken breasts over, and liberally spray with cooking spray again; cook another 6 minutes. Once golden brown, check for an internal temperature of 75°C.

Chapter 7
Beef, Pork & Lamb Recipes

Simple BBQ Baby Pork Ribs
Prep time: 10 minutes | Cook time: 30 minutes | Serves 6

- 1 rack baby back ribs
- 240g BBQ sauce
- 90g BBQ rub
- 240ml water

1. In a bowl, mix together BBQ sauce, BBQ rub and water.
2. Add the pork ribs and coat with the mixture generously.
3. Refrigerate to marinate for about 20 minutes.
4. Grease basket of Ninja Foodi 2-Basket Air Fryer.
5. Press your chosen zone - "Zone 1" or "Zone 2" and then rotate the knob to select "Air Fry".
6. Set the temperature to 180 degrees C and then set the time for 5 minutes to preheat.
7. After preheating, arrange the ribs into the basket of each zone.
8. Slide the basket into the Air Fryer and set the time for 30 minutes.
9. While cooking, flip the ribs once halfway through.
10. After cooking time is completed, remove the ribs from Air Fryer and place onto serving plates.
11. Serve and enjoy!

Simple Lamb Loin Chops
Prep time: 10 minutes | Cook time: 13 minutes | Serves 2

- 4 (50g, 1 cm thick) lamb loin chops
- 2 garlic cloves, crushed
- 1 teaspoon chili powder
- 2 teaspoons fresh rosemary, minced
- Salt and ground black pepper, as required

1. In a large bowl, place all ingredients and mix well.
2. Refrigerate to marinate overnight.
3. Remove chops from bowl and season with a little salt.
4. Grease either basket of "Zone 1" or "Zone 2" of Ninja Foodi 2-Basket Air Fryer.
5. Press your chosen zone - "Zone 1" or "Zone 2" and then rotate the knob for the zone to select "Bake".
6. Set the temperature to 200 degrees C and then set the time for 5 minutes to preheat.
7. Rub the lamb chops with salt and black pepper generously.
8. After preheating, arrange lamb chops into the basket.
9. Slide basket into Air Fryer and set the time for 11 minutes.
10. Flip the chops once halfway through.
11. After cooking time is completed, remove the chops from Air Fryer and serve hot.

T-bone Steak With Roasted Tomato, Corn And Asparagus Salsa
Prep time: 5 minutes | Cook time: 15-20 minutes | Serves 2

- 1 (20-ounce) T-bone steak
- salt and freshly ground black pepper
- Salsa
- 1½ cups cherry tomatoes
- ¾ cup sweetcorn kernels (fresh, or frozen and thawed)
- 1½ cups sliced asparagus (1-inch slices) (about ½ bunch)
- 1 tablespoon + 1 teaspoon olive oil, divided
- salt and freshly ground black pepper
- 1½ teaspoons red wine vinegar
- 3 tablespoons chopped fresh basil
- 1 tablespoon chopped fresh chives

1. Preheat the air fryer to 200°C.
2. Season the steak with salt and pepper and air-fry at 200°C for 10 minutes (medium-rare), 12 minutes (medium), or 15 minutes (well-done), flipping the steak once halfway through the cooking time.
3. In the meantime, toss the tomatoes, corn and asparagus in a bowl with a teaspoon or so of olive oil, salt and freshly ground black pepper.
4. When the steak has finished cooking, remove it to a cutting board, tent loosely with foil and let it rest. Transfer the vegetables to the air fryer and air-fry at 200°C for 5 minutes, shaking the basket once or twice during the cooking process. Transfer the cooked vegetables back into the bowl and toss with the red wine vinegar, remaining olive oil and fresh herbs.
5. To serve, slice the steak on the bias and serve with some of the salsa on top.

Filet Mignon Wrapped in Bacon
Prep time: 10 minutes | Cook time: 15 minutes | Serves 2

- 2 (50g) filet mignon
- 2 bacon slices
- Olive oil cooking spray
- Salt and ground black pepper, as required

1. Wrap 1 bacon slice around each filet mignon and secure with toothpicks.
2. Season the filets with salt and black pepper lightly.
3. Grease basket of Ninja Foodi 2-Basket Air Fryer.
4. Press your chosen zone - "Zone 1" or "Zone 2" and then rotate the knob to select "Air Fry".
5. Set the temperature to 200 degrees C and then set the time for 5 minutes to preheat.
6. After preheating, arrange the filets into the basket of each zone.
7. Slide the basket into the Air Fryer and set the time for 15 minutes.
8. While cooking, flip the filets once halfway through.
9. After cooking time is completed, remove the filets from Air Fryer and serve hot.

Taco Seasoned Steak
Prep time: 10 minutes | Cook time: 30 minutes | Serves 6

- 1 (455g) flank steaks
- 1½ tablespoons taco seasoning rub

1. Grease either basket of "Zone 1" or "Zone 2" of Ninja Foodi 2-Basket Air Fryer.
2. Press your chosen zone - "Zone 1" or "Zone 2" and then rotate the knob for the zone to select "Bake".
3. Set the temperature to 215 degrees C and then set the time for 5 minutes to preheat.
4. Rub the steaks with taco seasoning evenly.
5. After preheating, arrange the steak into the basket.
6. Slide basket into Air Fryer and set the time for 30 minutes.
7. After cooking time is completed, remove the steaks from Air Fryer and place onto a cutting board for about 10-15 minutes before slicing.
8. With a sharp knife, cut steak into desired size slices and serve.

Crispy Pierogi With Kielbasa And Onions
Prep time: 5 minutes | Cook time: 20 minutes | Serves 3

- 6 Frozen potato and cheese pierogi, thawed (about 12 pierogi to 1 pound)
- 225g Smoked kielbasa, sliced into 1.25 cm thick rounds
- 150g Sweet onion, very roughly chopped, preferably Vidalia
- Vegetable oil spray

1. Preheat the air fryer to 190°C (375°F).
2. In a large bowl, combine the pierogi, kielbasa rounds, and onion. Coat them with vegetable oil spray, toss well, spray again, and toss until everything is glistening.
3. When the air fryer is at temperature, transfer the contents of the bowl into the basket. (Items may be leaning against each other and even on top of each other.) Air-fry, tossing and rearranging everything twice so that all covered surfaces get exposed, for 20 minutes, or until the sausages have begun to brown and the pierogi are crisp.
4. Pour the contents of the basket onto a serving platter. Wait a minute or two just to take make sure nothing's searing hot before serving.

Honey Mesquite Pork Chops

Prep time: 5 minutes | Cook time: 10 minutes | Serves 2

- 2 tablespoons mesquite seasoning
- 60ml honey
- 1 tablespoon olive oil
- 1 tablespoon water
- Freshly ground black pepper
- 2 bone-in center cut pork chops

1. Whisk the mesquite seasoning, honey, olive oil, water and freshly ground black pepper together in a shallow glass dish. Pierce the chops all over and on both sides with a fork or meat tenderizer. Add the pork chops to the marinade and massage the marinade into the chops. Cover and marinate for 30 minutes.
2. Preheat the air fryer to 165°C.
3. Transfer the pork chops to the air fryer basket and pour half of the marinade over the chops, reserving the remaining marinade. Air-fry the pork chops for 6 minutes. Flip the pork chops over and pour the remaining marinade on top. Air-fry for an additional 3 minutes at 165°C. Then, increase the air fryer temperature to 200°C and air-fry the pork chops for an additional minute.
4. Transfer the pork chops to a serving plate, and let them rest for 5 minutes before serving. If you'd like a sauce for these chops, pour the cooked marinade from the bottom of the air fryer over the top.

Air Fried Steak

Prep time: 5 minutes | Cook time: 10 minutes | Serves 4

- 2 sirloin steaks
- 2 tsp rapeseed oil
- 2 tbsp steak seasoning
- Pepper
- Salt

1. Preheat the air fryer to 180°C/350°F.
2. Brush steak with rapeseed oil and season with steak seasoning, pepper, and salt.
3. Spray air fryer basket with cooking spray and place steak in the air fryer basket.
4. Cook for 10 minutes. Turn halfway through.
5. Slice and serve.

Lemon-Butter Veal Cutlets

Prep time: 5 minutes | Cook time: 4 minutes | Serves 2

- 3 strips Butter
- 3 Thinly pounded 2-ounce veal leg cutlets (less than ¼ inch thick)
- ¼ teaspoon Lemon-pepper seasoning

1. Preheat the air fryer to 200°C (400°F).
2. Run a vegetable peeler lengthwise along a hard, cold stick of butter, making 2, 3, or 4 long strips as the recipe requires for the number of cutlets you're making.
3. Lay the veal cutlets on a clean, dry cutting board or work surface. Sprinkle about 1/8 teaspoon of lemon-pepper seasoning over each. Set a strip of butter on top of each cutlet.
4. When the machine is at temperature, set the topped cutlets in the basket so that they don't overlap or even touch. Air-fry undisturbed for 4 minutes without turning.
5. Use a nonstick-safe spatula to transfer the cutlets to a serving plate or plates, taking care to keep as much of the butter on top as possible. Remove the basket from the drawer or from over the baking tray. Carefully pour the browned butter over the cutlets.

Marinated Rib-Eye Steak With Herb Roasted Mushrooms

Prep time: 5 minutes | Cook time: 10-15 minutes | Serves 2

- 2 tablespoons Worcestershire sauce
- 80ml red wine
- 2 (227g) boneless rib-eye steaks
- coarsely ground black pepper
- 227g chestnut mushrooms, stems trimmed and caps halved
- 2 tablespoons olive oil
- 1 teaspoon dried parsley
- 1 teaspoon fresh thyme leaves
- salt and freshly ground black pepper
- chopped fresh chives or parsley

1. Combine the Worcestershire sauce and red wine in a shallow baking dish. Add the steaks to the marinade, pierce them several times with the tines of a fork or a meat tenderizer and season them generously with the coarsely ground black pepper. Flip the steaks over and pierce the other side in a similar fashion, seasoning again with the coarsely ground black pepper. Marinate the steaks for 2 hours.
2. Preheat the oven to 200°C/180°C fan/gas mark 6.
3. Toss the mushrooms in a bowl with the olive oil, dried parsley, thyme, salt and freshly ground black pepper. Transfer the steaks from the marinade to a roasting tray, season with salt and scatter the mushrooms on top.
4. Roast the steaks and mushrooms in the preheated oven for 10 minutes for medium-rare, 12 minutes for medium, or 15 minutes for well-done, flipping the steaks once halfway through the cooking time.
5. Serve the steaks and mushrooms together with the chives or parsley sprinkled on top. A good steak sauce or some horseradish would be a nice accompaniment.

Kielbasa Sausage with Pineapple and Peppers

Prep time: 5 minutes | Cook time:10minutes |Serves2

- 340g kielbasa sausage
- 1 cup bell pepper chunks (any color)
- 1 can (227g) pineapple chunks in juice, drained
- 1 tablespoon barbeque seasoning
- 1 tablespoon soy sauce
- Cooking spray

1. Cut the kielbasa sausage into 1 cm slices.
2. In a medium bowl, toss together the sausage, bell pepper chunks, pineapple chunks, barbeque seasoning, and soy sauce.
3. Spray the air fryer basket with cooking spray.
4. Pour the sausage mixture into the basket.
5. Cook at 200°C for approximately 5 minutes. Shake the basket and cook for an additional 5 minutes.

Hot Dogs Wrapped in Bacon

Prep time: 10 minutes | Cook time: 15 minutes | Serves 2

- 2 bacon strips
- 2 hot dogs
- Salt and black pepper, to taste

1. Wrap each hot dog with bacon strip and season with salt and black pepper.
2. Grease basket of Ninja Foodi 2-Basket Air Fryer.
3. Press your chosen zone - "Zone 1" or "Zone 2" and then rotate the knob to select "Air Fry".
4. Set the temperature to 200 degrees C and then set the time for 5 minutes to preheat.
5. After preheating, arrange bacon wrapped hot dogs into the basket of each zone.
6. Slide the basket into the Air Fryer and set the time for 15 minutes.
7. While cooking, flip the hot dogs once halfway through.
8. After cooking time is completed, remove the filets from Air Fryer and serve hot.

Pork Belly Marinated In Onion-coconut Cream

Prep time: 5 minutes | Cook time: 25 minutes | Serves 3

- ½ pork belly, sliced into thin strips
- 1 onion, finely chopped
- 1 tablespoon butter
- 4 tablespoons coconut cream
- Salt and pepper to taste

1. In a mixing bowl, combine the pork belly, onion, butter, coconut cream, salt and pepper. Allow to marinate in the fridge for 2 hours.
2. Preheat the air fryer to 180°C (356°F).
3. Place the pork strips in the air fryer and cook for 25 minutes at 180°C.

Italian Meatballs

Prep time: 5 minutes | Cook time: 12 minutes | Serves 8

- 340g lean minced beef
- 170g bulk mild or hot Italian sausage meat
- 60g seasoned Italian-style dried bread crumbs
- 1 large egg
- 3 tablespoons whole or low-fat milk
- Olive oil spray

1. Preheat the air fryer to 190°C (375°F).
2. In a mixing bowl, combine the minced beef, Italian sausage meat, bread crumbs, egg, and milk until well combined. Using clean hands, shape the mixture into large meatballs, using about 1/4 cup for each. Place the meatballs on a large cutting board and spray them on all sides with olive oil spray. Be careful when handling them as they can be fragile.
3. Once the air fryer has reached the desired temperature, place the meatballs in the basket with enough space between them to avoid touching, even if there is only a fraction of an inch between them. Air-fry for 12 minutes without disturbing, or until an instant-read meat thermometer inserted into the center of a meatball registers 74°C (165°F).
4. Use kitchen tongs to gently transfer the meatballs to a serving platter or cutting board. Allow them to cool for a few minutes before serving.

Greek-style Pork Stuffed Jalapeño Poppers

Prep time: 5 minutes | Cook time: 30 minutes | Serves 6

- 6 jalapeños, halved lengthwise
- 3 tbsp diced Kalamata olives
- 3 tbsp olive oil
- 115g ground pork
- 2 tbsp feta cheese
- 28g cream cheese, softened
- ½ tsp dried mint
- 120g Greek yogurt

1. Warm 2 tbsp of olive oil in a frying pan over medium heat.
2. Add the ground pork and cook for 6 minutes until it is no longer pink.
3. Preheat the air fryer to 180°C (350°F).
4. In a mixing bowl, combine the cooked pork, olives, feta cheese, and cream cheese.
5. Stuff the jalapeño halves with the pork mixture.
6. Place the stuffed jalapeños in the air fryer basket and air-fry for 6 minutes.
7. In a small bowl, mix the Greek yogurt with the remaining olive oil and dried mint.
8. Serve the jalapeño poppers hot, with the minted Greek yogurt as a dipping sauce.

Sweet Potato-Crusted Pork Rib Chops

Prep time: 5 minutes | Cook time: 14 minutes | Serves 2

- 2 Large egg white(s), well beaten
- 1½ cups (about 6 ounces) Crushed sweet potato chips (certified gluten-free, if a concern)
- 1 teaspoon Ground cinnamon
- 1 teaspoon Ground dried ginger
- 1 teaspoon Table salt (optional)
- 2 10-ounce, 1-inch-thick bone-in pork rib chop(s)

1. Preheat the air fryer to 190°C/375°F/Gas Mark 5.
2. Set up and fill two shallow soup plates or small pie plates on your counter: one for the beaten egg white(s); and one for the crushed chips, mixed with the cinnamon, ginger, and salt (if using).
3. Dip a chop in the egg white(s), coating it on both sides as well as the edges. Let the excess egg white slip back into the rest, then set it in the crushed chip mixture. Turn it several times, pressing gently, until evenly coated on both sides and the edges. If necessary, set the chop aside and coat the remaining chop(s).
4. Set the chop(s) in the basket with as much air space between them as possible. Air-fry undisturbed for 12 minutes, or until crunchy and browned and an instant-read meat thermometer inserted into the center of a chop (without touching bone) registers 63°C/145°F. If the machine is at 180°C/360°F/Gas Mark 4, you may need to add 2 minutes to the cooking time.
5. Use kitchen tongs to transfer the chop(s) to a wire rack. Cool for 2 or 3 minutes before serving.

Bacon Wrapped Filets Mignons

Prep time: 5 minutes | Cook time: 18 minutes | Serves 4

- 4 rashers of streaky bacon
- 4 (8-ounce) fillet steaks
- 1 tablespoon fresh thyme leaves
- salt and freshly ground black pepper

1. Preheat the air fryer to 200°C/400°F.
2. Lay the bacon slices down on a cutting board and sprinkle the thyme leaves on the bacon slices. Remove any string tying the fillet steaks and place the steaks down on their sides on top of the bacon slices. Roll the bacon around the side of the fillets and secure the bacon to the fillets with a toothpick or two.
3. Season the steaks generously with salt and freshly ground black pepper and transfer the steaks to the air fryer.
4. Air-fry for 18 minutes, turning the steaks over halfway through the cooking process. This should cook your steaks to about medium, depending on how thick they are. If you'd prefer your steaks medium-rare or medium-well, simply add or subtract two minutes from the cooking time. Remove the steaks from the air fryer and let them rest for 5 minutes before removing the toothpicks and serving. (Just enough time to quickly air-fry some vegetables to go with them!)

California Burritos

Prep time: 5 minutes | Cook time: 17 minutes | Serves 4

- 454g sirloin steak, sliced thin
- 1 teaspoon dried oregano
- 1 teaspoon ground cumin
- ½ teaspoon garlic powder
- 16 potato croquettes
- 85g sour cream
- ½ lime, juiced
- 2 tablespoons hot sauce
- 1 large avocado, pitted
- 1 teaspoon salt, divided
- 4 large (8- to 10-inch) flour tortillas
- 120g shredded cheddar cheese or Monterey jack
- 2 tablespoons avocado oil

1. Preheat the air fryer to 190°C.
2. Season the steak with oregano, cumin, and garlic powder. Place the steak on one side of the air fryer and the potato croquettes on the other side. (It's okay for them to touch, because the flavors will all come together in the burrito.) Cook for 8 minutes, toss, and cook an additional 4 to 6 minutes.
3. Meanwhile, in a small bowl, stir together the sour cream, lime juice, and hot sauce.
4. In another small bowl, mash together the avocado and season with ½ teaspoon of the salt, to taste.
5. To assemble the burrito, lay out the tortillas, equally divide the meat amongst the tortillas. Season the steak equally with the remaining ½ teaspoon salt. Then layer the mashed avocado and sour cream mixture on top. Top each tortilla with 4 potato croquettes and finish each with 2 tablespoons cheese. Roll up the sides and, while holding in the sides, roll up the burrito. Place the burritos in the air fryer basket and brush with avocado oil (working in batches as needed); cook for 3 minutes or until lightly golden on the outside.

Chapter 8
Vegetarians Recipes

Pepper-Pineapple With Butter-Sugar Glaze

Prep time: 5 minutes | Cook time: 10 minutes | Serves 2

- 1 medium-sized pineapple, peeled and sliced
- 1 red bell pepper, seeded and thinly sliced
- 1 teaspoon demerara sugar
- 2 teaspoons melted butter
- Salt to taste

1. Preheat the air fryer to 200°C/400°F/Gas Mark 6.
2. Place the grill pan accessory in the air fryer.
3. Mix all the ingredients in a bowl and toss well to coat the pineapple and peppers evenly.
4. Transfer the mixture onto the grill pan and cook for 10 minutes, flipping the pineapple and peppers every 5 minutes, until the pineapple is slightly caramelised and the peppers are tender.
5. Serve the Pepper-Pineapple With Butter-Sugar Glaze hot as a side dish or as a topping for grilled chicken or fish.

Baked Polenta With Chili-cheese

Prep time: 5 minutes | Cook time: 10 minutes | Serves 3

- 1 commercial polenta roll, sliced
- 240ml cheddar cheese sauce
- 1 tablespoon chili powder

1. Place the baking dish accessory in the air fryer.
2. Arrange the polenta slices in the baking dish.
3. Add the chili powder and cheddar cheese sauce.
4. Close the air fryer and cook for 10 minutes at 200°C/400°F/Gas Mark 6.

Twice-Baked Broccoli-Cheddar Potatoes

Prep time: 5 minutes | Cook time: 35 minutes | Serves 4

- 4 large baking potatoes
- 2 tablespoons plus 2 teaspoons of ranch dressing
- 1 teaspoon of salt
- 1/2 teaspoon of ground black pepper
- 1/4 cup of chopped cooked broccoli florets
- 1 cup of grated mature cheddar cheese

1. Preheat the air fryer to 200°C/400°F.
2. Prick the potatoes with a fork several times, place them in the air fryer basket, and cook for 30 minutes until they are tender when pierced with a fork.
3. Once the potatoes have cooled enough to handle, slice them lengthwise and scoop out the potato flesh into a large bowl, making sure to keep the potato skins intact.
4. Add ranch dressing, salt, pepper, broccoli, and cheddar to the potato flesh and stir until well combined.
5. Spoon the potato mixture back into the potato skins and return them to the air fryer basket. Cook for an additional 5 minutes until the cheese is melted and the potatoes are heated through.
6. Serve hot.

Italian Seasoned Easy Pasta Chips

Prep time: 5 minutes | Cook time: 10 minutes | Serves 2

- ½ teaspoon salt
- 1 ½ teaspoon Italian seasoning blend
- 1 tablespoon nutritional yeast
- 1 tablespoon olive oil
- 200g whole wheat bowtie pasta

1. Place the baking dish accessory in the air fryer and preheat it to 200°C/400°F/Gas Mark 6.
2. Cook the pasta in salted boiling water until al dente, then drain and rinse under cold water to stop the cooking process.
3. In a bowl, toss the cooked pasta with Italian seasoning blend, nutritional yeast, and olive oil until evenly coated.
4. Transfer the pasta to the baking dish and spread it out evenly.
5. Close the air fryer and cook for 10 minutes at 200°C/400°F/Gas Mark 6, shaking the basket every 5 minutes to ensure even cooking, until the pasta chips are golden and crispy.
6. Serve the Italian Seasoned Easy Pasta Chips hot as a snack or appetizer with a dipping sauce of your choice.

Home-Style Cinnamon Rolls

Prep time: 5 minutes | Cook time: 40 minutes | Serves 4

- 250g pizza dough
- 80g dark brown sugar
- 55g butter, softened
- 1/2 tsp ground cinnamon

1. Preheat air fryer to 180°C. Roll out the dough into a rectangle. Using a knife, spread the brown sugar and butter, covering all the edges, and sprinkle with cinnamon.
2. Fold the long side of the dough into a log, then cut it into 8 equal pieces, avoiding compression. Place the rolls, spiral-side up, onto a parchment-lined sheet. Let rise for 20 minutes.
3. Grease the rolls with cooking spray and bake for 8 minutes until golden brown. Serve right away.

Charred Cauliflower Tacos

Prep time: 5 minutes | Cook time: 10 minutes | Serves 4

- 1 head of cauliflower, washed and cut into florets
- 2 tablespoons of rapeseed oil
- 2 teaspoons of taco seasoning
- 1 medium avocado
- ½ teaspoon of garlic powder
- ¼ teaspoon of black pepper
- ¼ teaspoon of salt
- 2 tablespoons of chopped red onion
- 2 teaspoons of fresh squeezed lime juice
- ¼ cup of chopped coriander
- Eight 6-inch corn tortillas
- ½ cup of cooked sweetcorn
- ½ cup of shredded red cabbage

1. Preheat the oven to 200°C/180°C fan/gas mark 6.
2. In a large bowl, toss the cauliflower with the rapeseed oil and taco seasoning. Spread the cauliflower out onto a baking sheet and roast in the preheated oven for 10 minutes, or until tender and lightly charred.
3. While the cauliflower is roasting, prepare the avocado sauce. In a medium bowl, mash the avocado; then mix in the garlic powder, black pepper, salt, and red onion. Stir in the lime juice and coriander; set aside.
4. Remove the cauliflower from the oven.
5. Place 1 tablespoon of avocado sauce in the middle of a tortilla, and top with sweetcorn, red cabbage, and charred cauliflower. Repeat with the remaining tortillas.
6. Serve immediately and enjoy your delicious British-style Charred Cauliflower Tacos!

Chicano Rice Bowls

Prep time: 10 minutes | Cook time: 10 minutes | Serves 4

- 240g sour cream
- 2 tbsp milk
- 1 tsp ground cumin
- 1 tsp chili powder
- 1/8 tsp cayenne pepper
- 1 tbsp tomato puree
- 1 white onion, chopped
- 1 clove garlic, minced
- ½ tsp ground turmeric
- ½ tsp salt
- 240g canned black beans
- 240g canned sweetcorn
- 1 tsp olive oil
- 360g cooked brown rice
- 3 tomatoes, diced
- 1 avocado, diced

1. Whisk the sour cream, milk, cumin, ground turmeric, chili powder, cayenne pepper, and salt in a bowl. Let chill covered in the fridge until ready to use.
2. Preheat air fryer at 180°C. Combine beans, white onion, tomato puree, garlic, sweetcorn, and olive oil in a bowl. Transfer it into the frying basket and Air Fry for 5 minutes. Divide cooked rice into 4 serving bowls. Top each with bean mixture, tomatoes, and avocado and drizzle with sour cream mixture over. Serve immediately.

Brussels Sprouts With Balsamic Oil

Prep time: 5 minutes | Cook time: 15 minutes | Serves 4

- ¼ teaspoon salt
- 1 tablespoon balsamic vinegar
- 500g Brussels sprouts, halved
- 2 tablespoons olive oil

1. Preheat the air fryer to 200°C/400°F/Gas Mark 6 for 5 minutes.
2. Mix all the ingredients in a bowl until the Brussels sprouts are well coated with the balsamic oil mixture.
3. Place the Brussels sprouts in the air fryer basket.
4. Close the air fryer and cook for 15 minutes at 200°C/400°F/Gas Mark 6, until the Brussels sprouts are crispy and tender.
5. Serve the Brussels Sprouts With Balsamic Oil hot as a side dish with roasted meats or as a topping for salads.

Spicy Sesame Tempeh Slaw With Peanut Dressing

Prep time: 10 minutes | Cook time: 8 minutes | Serves 2

- 475ml hot water
- 1 teaspoon salt
- 225g tempeh, sliced into 2.5cm-long pieces
- 2 tablespoons low-sodium soy sauce
- 2 tablespoons rice vinegar
- 1 tablespoon filtered water
- 2 teaspoons sesame oil
- ½ teaspoon fresh ginger
- 1 clove garlic, minced
- ¼ teaspoon black pepper
- ½ jalapeño, sliced
- 300g cabbage slaw
- 4 tablespoons Peanut Dressing (see the following recipe)
- 2 tablespoons fresh chopped coriander
- 2 tablespoons chopped peanuts

1. Mix the hot water with the salt and pour over the tempeh in a glass bowl. Stir and cover with a tea towel for 10 minutes.
2. Drain the water and leave the tempeh in the bowl.
3. In a medium bowl, mix the soy sauce, rice vinegar, filtered water, sesame oil, ginger, garlic, pepper, and jalapeño. Pour over the tempeh and cover with a tea towel. Place in the refrigerator to marinate for at least 2 hours.
4. Preheat the air fryer to 190°C. Remove the tempeh from the bowl and discard the remaining marinade.
5. Spray the metal trivet that goes into the air fryer basket with cooking spray and place the tempeh on top of the trivet.
6. Cook for 4 minutes, flip, and cook another 4 minutes.
7. In a large bowl, mix the cabbage slaw with the Peanut Dressing and toss in the coriander and chopped peanuts.
8. Divide onto 4 plates and place the cooked tempeh on top when cooking completes. Serve immediately.

Sweet And Spicy Barbecue Tofu

Prep time: 5 minutes | Cook time: 1 Hour 15 Minutes | Serves 4

- 1 block (400g) of extra-firm tofu, drained
- 120ml barbecue sauce
- 70g brown sugar
- 1 teaspoon liquid smoke
- 1 teaspoon crushed red pepper flakes
- ½ teaspoon salt
- Cooking spray

1. Press the tofu block to remove excess moisture. If you don't have a tofu press, line a baking sheet with paper towels and set the tofu on top. Set a second baking sheet on top of the tofu and weight it with a heavy item such as a skillet. Let the tofu sit for at least 30 minutes, changing the paper towels if necessary.
2. Cut the pressed tofu into 24 equal pieces and set aside.
3. In a large bowl, combine barbecue sauce, brown sugar, liquid smoke, red pepper flakes, and salt. Mix well and add the tofu, coating completely. Cover and let marinate for at least 30 minutes on the counter.
4. Preheat the air fryer to 200°C/400°F/Gas Mark 6.
5. Spray the air fryer basket with cooking spray and add the marinated tofu. Cook for 15 minutes, shaking the basket twice during cooking.
6. Let the tofu cool for 10 minutes before serving warm.

Mushroom Bolognese Casserole
Prep time: 5 minutes | Cook time: 20 minutes | Serves 4

- 1 cup tinned chopped tomatoes
- 2 garlic cloves, minced
- 1 tsp onion powder
- ¾ tsp dried basil
- ¾ tsp dried oregano
- 1 cup chopped mushrooms
- 16 oz cooked spaghetti

1. Preheat the oven to 200°C/180°C fan/gas mark 6.
2. Mix the tinned chopped tomatoes and their juices, minced garlic, onion powder, dried basil, dried oregano, and chopped mushrooms in a baking dish.
3. Cover with aluminum foil and bake for 6 minutes.
4. Remove the dish from the oven and add the cooked spaghetti; stir to coat.
5. Cover with aluminum foil and bake for an additional 3 minutes, until bubbly.
6. Serve and enjoy!

Meatless Kimchi Bowls
Prep time: 5 minutes | Cook time: 20 minutes | Serves 4

- 2 cups of canned chickpeas
- 1 carrot, julienned
- 6 spring onions, sliced
- 1 courgette, diced
- 2 tbsp of soy sauce
- 2 tsp of sesame oil
- 1 tsp of rice vinegar
- 2 tsp of granulated sugar
- 1 tbsp of gochujang
- ¼ tsp of salt
- ½ cup of kimchi
- 2 tsp of roasted sesame seeds

1. Preheat the oven to 180°C/160°C fan/gas mark 4.
2. In a baking pan, combine all ingredients except for the kimchi, 2 spring onions, and sesame seeds.
3. Place the pan in the preheated oven and bake for 15-20 minutes until vegetables are tender.
4. Toss in the kimchi and bake for an additional 2-3 minutes.
5. Divide the mixture between 4 bowls and garnish with the remaining spring onions and sesame seeds.
6. Serve immediately and enjoy your delicious British-style Meatless Kimchi Bowls!

Rigatoni With Roasted Onions, Fennel, Spinach And Lemon Pepper Ricotta
Prep time: 5 minutes | Cook time: 13 minutes | Serves 2

- 1 red onion, rough chopped into large chunks
- 2 teaspoons olive oil, divided
- 1 bulb fennel, sliced 0.6cm thick
- 170g ricotta cheese
- 1½ teaspoons finely chopped lemon zest, plus more for garnish
- 1 teaspoon lemon juice
- salt and freshly ground black pepper
- 227g (½ pound) dried rigatoni pasta
- 85g baby spinach leaves

1. Bring a large saucepan of salted water to a boil on the stovetop and Preheat the air fryer to 200°C.
2. While the water is coming to a boil, toss the chopped onion in 1 teaspoon of olive oil and transfer to the air fryer basket. Air-fry at 200°C for 5 minutes. Toss the sliced fennel with 1 teaspoon of olive oil and add this to the air fryer basket with the onions. Continue to air-fry at 200°C for 8 minutes, shaking the basket a few times during the cooking process.
3. Combine the ricotta cheese, lemon zest and juice, ¼ teaspoon of salt and freshly ground black pepper in a bowl and stir until smooth.
4. Add the dried rigatoni to the boiling water and cook according to the package directions. When the pasta is cooked al dente, reserve one cup of the pasta water and drain the pasta into a colander.
5. Place the spinach in a serving bowl and immediately transfer the hot pasta to the bowl, wilting the spinach. Add the roasted onions and fennel and toss together. Add a little pasta water to the dish if it needs moistening. Then, dollop the lemon pepper ricotta cheese on top and nestle it into the hot pasta. Garnish with more lemon zest if desired.

Chapter 9
Vegetable Side Dishes Recipes

Grilled Cheese

Prep time: 5 minutes | Cook time: 25 minutes | Serves 2

- 4 slices of bread
- 1 cup grated cheddar cheese
- 50g butter, softened

1. Preheat the Air Fryer at 180°C (356°F).
2. Put the cheese and butter in separate bowls.
3. Apply the butter to each side of the bread slices with a brush.
4. Spread the grated cheese across two of the slices of bread and make two sandwiches. Transfer both to the fryer.
5. Cook for 5 – 7 minutes or until a golden brown color is achieved and the cheese is melted.
6. Serve immediately.

Caraway Seed Pretzel Sticks

Prep time: 5 minutes | Cook time 30 minutes | Serves 4

- ½ pizza dough
- 1 tsp bicarbonate of soda
- 2 tbsp caraway seeds
- 240 ml hot water
- Cooking spray

1. Preheat air fryer to 200°C/400°F.
2. Roll out the pizza dough on a sheet of parchment paper into a rectangle and cut into 8 strips.
3. In a bowl, whisk the bicarbonate of soda and hot water until dissolved.
4. Submerge each strip of dough in the mixture, shake off any excess, and stretch them 1-2 inches longer.
5. Scatter caraway seeds over the strips and let them rise for 10 minutes in the air fryer basket.
6. Grease the strips with cooking spray and air fry for 8 minutes, turning once, until they are golden brown.
7. Serve the pretzel sticks immediately.

Zucchini Fries

Prep time: 10 minutes | Cook time: 12 minutes | Serves 3

- 1 large courgette
- 75g All-purpose flour or tapioca flour
- 2 Large egg(s), well beaten
- 75g Seasoned Italian-style dried bread crumbs (gluten-free, if a concern)
- Olive oil spray

1. Preheat the air fryer to 200°C.
2. Trim the courgette into a long rectangular block, taking off the ends and four "sides" to make this shape. Cut the block lengthwise into 1cm-thick slices. Lay these slices flat and cut in half widthwise. Slice each of these pieces into 1cm-thick batons.
3. Set up and fill three shallow soup plates or small pie plates on your counter: one for the flour, one for the beaten egg(s), and one for the bread crumbs.
4. Set a courgette baton in the flour and turn it several times to coat all sides. Gently shake off any excess flour, then dip it in the egg(s), turning it to coat. Let any excess egg slip back into the rest, then set the baton in the bread crumbs and turn it several times, pressing gently to coat all sides, even the ends. Set aside on a cutting board and continue coating the remainder of the batons in the same way.
5. Lightly coat the batons on all sides with olive oil spray. Set them in two flat layers in the basket, the top layer at a 90-degree angle to the bottom one, with a little air space between the batons in each layer. In the end, the whole thing will look like a crosshatch pattern. Air-fry undisturbed for 6 minutes.
6. Use kitchen tongs to gently rearrange the batons so that any covered parts are now uncovered. The batons no longer need to be in a crosshatch pattern. Continue air-frying undisturbed for 6 minutes, or until lightly browned and crisp.
7. Gently pour the contents of the basket onto a wire rack. Spread the batons out and cool for only a minute or two before serving.

Roasted Asparagus

Prep time: 5 minutes | Cook time: 12 minutes | Serves 4

- 1 tablespoon olive oil
- 1 pound asparagus spears, ends trimmed
- ¼ teaspoon salt
- ¼ teaspoon ground black pepper
- 1 tablespoon salted butter, melted

1. Preheat the air fryer to 190°C.
2. In a large bowl, toss the asparagus spears with olive oil, salt, and pepper until well coated.
3. Place the asparagus spears in the air fryer basket in a single layer. Cook for 12 minutes, shaking the basket halfway through cooking, until the asparagus is tender and lightly browned.
4. Transfer the roasted asparagus to a serving dish and drizzle with melted butter. Serve immediately.

Balsamic Green Beans With Bacon

Prep time: 5 minutes | Cook time: 15minutes | Serves 4

- 300g green beans, trimmed
- 15g butter, melted
- Salt and pepper to taste
- 1 bacon slice, diced
- 1 clove garlic, minced
- 15ml balsamic vinegar

1. Preheat the air fryer to 190°C (375°F).
2. In a bowl, combine the green beans, melted butter, salt, and pepper.
3. Place the green bean mixture in the air fryer basket and air fry for 5 minutes.
4. Stir in the diced bacon and air fry for 4 more minutes.
5. Mix in the minced garlic and air fry for 1 minute.
6. Transfer the green bean mixture to a serving dish, drizzle with balsamic vinegar, and combine.
7. Serve immediately.

Cheesy Potato Pot

Prep time: 5 minutes | Cook time: 13 minutes | Serves 4

- 650g cubed red potatoes (unpeeled, cut into 1cm cubes)
- 1/2 teaspoon garlic powder
- Salt and pepper
- 1 tablespoon oil
- Chopped chives for garnish (optional)

SAUCE:
- 2 tablespoons milk
- 1 tablespoon butter
- 56g sharp Cheddar cheese, grated
- 1 tablespoon sour cream

1. Place potato cubes in a large bowl and sprinkle with garlic, salt, and pepper. Add oil and stir to coat well.
2. Preheat the oven to 200°C/400°F/Gas Mark 6. Transfer the potatoes to a baking dish and bake for 20-25 minutes or until tender, stirring occasionally.
3. While potatoes are cooking, combine milk and butter in a small saucepan. Warm over medium-low heat to melt butter. Add cheese and stir until it melts. The melted cheese will remain separated from the milk mixture. Remove from heat until potatoes are done.
4. When ready to serve, add sour cream to cheese mixture and stir over medium-low heat just until warmed.
5. Place cooked potatoes in a serving bowl. Pour the sauce over the potatoes and stir to combine.
6. Garnish with chives, if desired.

Tandoori Cauliflower

Prep time: 5 minutes | Cook time: 10 minutes | Serves 4

- 120ml plain full-fat yogurt (not Greek yogurt)
- 1½ teaspoons yellow curry powder, purchased or homemade
- 1½ teaspoons lemon juice
- ¾ teaspoon table salt (optional)
- 675g 2-inch cauliflower florets

1. Preheat the air fryer to 200°C.
2. In a large bowl, whisk together the yogurt, curry powder, lemon juice, and salt (if using) until the mixture is smooth. Add the cauliflower florets and gently stir until they are evenly coated with the yogurt mixture.
3. When the air fryer has reached temperature, transfer the cauliflower florets to the basket, spreading them out in a single layer as much as possible. Air-fry for 10 minutes, tossing and rearranging the florets twice during cooking so that any covered or touching parts are exposed to the hot air. The cauliflower should be lightly browned and tender but still a bit crunchy.
4. Remove the basket from the air fryer and transfer the cauliflower to a wire rack to cool for at least 5 minutes before serving. The cauliflower can be served warm or at room temperature.

Steakhouse Baked Potatoes

Prep time: 5 minutes | Cook time: 55 minutes | Serves 3

- 3 10-ounce Maris Piper potatoes
- 2 tablespoons Olive oil
- 1 teaspoon Table salt

1. Preheat the air fryer to 190°C (375°F).
2. Poke holes all over each potato with a fork. Rub the skin of each potato with 2 teaspoons of the olive oil, then sprinkle ¼ teaspoon salt all over each potato.
3. When the machine is at temperature, set the potatoes in the basket in one layer with as much air space between them as possible. Air-fry for 50 minutes, turning once, or until soft to the touch but with crunchy skins. If the machine is at 180°C (360°F), you may need to add up to 5 minutes to the cooking time.
4. Use kitchen tongs to gently transfer the baked potatoes to a wire rack. Cool for 5 or 10 minutes before serving.

Asparagus & Cherry Tomato Roast

Prep time: 5 minutes | Cook time: 20 minutes | Serves 6

- 2 tbsp dill, chopped
- 500g cherry tomatoes
- 680g asparagus, trimmed
- 2 tbsp olive oil
- 3 garlic cloves, minced
- 1/2 tsp salt

1. Preheat the oven to 200°C/400°F/Gas Mark 6.
2. In a bowl, add all the ingredients except for the dill and toss until the vegetables are well coated with the oil.
3. Transfer the vegetable mixture to a baking dish and roast for 15-20 minutes or until the vegetables are tender and lightly browned, stirring occasionally.
4. Serve topped with fresh dill.

Perfect Asparagus

Prep time: 15 minutes | Cook time: 10 minutes | Serves 3

- 450g very thin asparagus spears
- 2 tablespoons olive oil
- 1 teaspoon coarse sea salt or kosher salt
- 3/4 teaspoon finely grated lemon zest

1. Preheat the oven to 200°C/400°F/Gas Mark 6.
2. Trim just enough off the bottom of the asparagus spears so they'll fit in the baking tray. Put the spears on a large plate and drizzle them with some of the olive oil. Turn them over and drizzle more olive oil, working to get all the spears coated.
3. Place the asparagus spears in a single layer on a baking tray. Roast in the oven for 8-10 minutes, tossing and rearranging the spears once, until tender.
4. Transfer the roasted asparagus to a serving platter. Spread out the spears. Sprinkle them with the salt and lemon zest while still warm. Serve at once.

Mouth-Watering Provençal Mushrooms

Prep time: 5 minutes | Cook time: 35 minutes | Serves 4

- 900g mushrooms, quartered
- 2-3 tbsp olive oil
- 1/2 tsp garlic powder
- 2 tsp herbs de Provence
- 2 tbsp dry white wine

1. Preheat the oven to 180°C/350°F/Gas Mark 4.
2. In a bowl, mix together the olive oil, garlic powder, herbs de Provence, and white wine.
3. Add the mushrooms and toss gently to coat.
4. Transfer the mixture into a baking dish and bake for 25-30 minutes or until the mushrooms are tender and lightly browned, stirring occasionally.
5. Serve hot and enjoy!

Chili-Oiled Brussels Sprouts

Prep time: 5 minutes | Cook time: 30 minutes | Serves 4

- 250g Brussels sprouts, trimmed and halved
- 1 tsp olive oil
- 1 tsp chili oil
- Salt and pepper to taste

1. Preheat air fryer to 180°C.
2. In a bowl, mix together Brussels sprouts, olive oil, chili oil, salt, and pepper.
3. Transfer the mixture to the air fryer basket.
4. Cook for 20 minutes, shaking the basket a few times during cooking until the sprouts are crispy and golden brown on the outside, and tender on the inside.
5. Serve immediately and enjoy!

Sriracha Green Beans

Prep time: 5 minutes | Cook time: 30 minutes | Serves 4

- ½ tbsp toasted sesame seeds
- 1 tbsp soy sauce
- ½ tbsp Sriracha sauce
- 4 tsp rapeseed oil
- 340g trimmed green beans
- 1 tbsp coriander, chopped

1. Mix the soy sauce, Sriracha sauce, and 1 tsp of rapeseed oil in a small bowl.
2. In a large bowl, toss green beans with the remaining oil.
3. Preheat air fryer to 190°C (375°F).
4. Place the green beans in the frying basket and Air Fry for 8 minutes, shaking the basket once until the beans are charred and tender.
5. Toss the beans with sauce, coriander, and sesame seeds.
6. Serve.

Panzanella Salad With Crispy Croutons

Prep time: 10 minutes | Cook time: 3 minutes | Serves 4

- ½ French baguette, sliced in half lengthwise
- 2 large cloves garlic
- 2 large ripe tomatoes, divided
- 2 small cucumbers, quartered and diced
- ¼ cup black olives
- 1 tablespoon chopped, fresh oregano or 1 teaspoon dried oregano
- ¼ cup chopped fresh basil
- ¼ cup chopped fresh parsley
- ½ cup sliced red onion
- 2 tablespoons red wine vinegar
- ¼ cup extra-virgin olive oil
- Salt and pepper, to taste

1. Preheat the air fryer to 190°C.
2. Place the baguette into the air fryer and toast for 3 to 5 minutes or until lightly golden brown.
3. Remove the bread from the air fryer and immediately rub 1 raw garlic clove firmly onto the inside portion of each piece of bread, scraping the garlic onto the bread.
4. Slice 1 of the tomatoes in half and rub the cut edge of one half of the tomato onto the toasted bread. Season the rubbed bread with sea salt to taste.
5. Cut the bread into cubes and place in a large bowl. Cube the remaining 1½ tomatoes and add to the bowl. Add the cucumbers, olives, oregano, basil, parsley, and onion; stir to mix. Drizzle the red wine vinegar into the bowl, and stir. Drizzle the olive oil over the top, stir, and adjust the seasonings with salt and pepper.
6. Serve immediately or allow to sit at room temperature for up to 1 hour before serving.

Perfect Chips

Prep time: 5 minutes | Cook time: 37 minutes | Serves 3

- 1 pound large Maris Piper potatoes
- Vegetable oil or sunflower oil spray
- ½ teaspoon Table salt

1. Peel the potatoes and cut them lengthwise into ¼-inch-thick slices, then cut each slice into ¼-inch-thick matchsticks.
2. Rinse the potato matchsticks in a bowl of cold water and soak for 5 minutes. Drain in a colander set in the sink, then pat them dry with paper towels.
3. Preheat the air fryer to 110°C (or 230°F, if that's the closest setting).
4. When the machine is at temperature, arrange the matchsticks in an even layer (if overlapping but not compact) in the basket. Air-fry for 20 minutes, tossing and rearranging the chips twice.
5. Pour the contents of the basket into a big bowl. Increase the air fryer's temperature to 165°C (or 330°F, if that's the closest setting).
6. Generously coat the chips with vegetable or sunflower oil spray. Toss well, then coat them again to make sure they're covered on all sides, tossing (and maybe spraying) a couple of times to make sure.
7. When the machine is at temperature, pour the chips into the basket and air-fry for 12 minutes, tossing and rearranging the chips at least twice.
8. Increase the machine's temperature to 190°C (or 375°F or 380°F, if one of these is the closest setting). Air-fry for 5 minutes more (from the moment you raise the temperature), tossing and rearranging the chips at least twice to keep them from burning and to make sure they all get an even measure of the heat, until golden brown and crispy.
9. Pour the contents of the basket into a serving bowl. Toss the chips with the salt and serve hot.

Chapter 10
Holiday Specials

Lush Snack Mix

Prep time: 10 minutes | Cook time: 10 minutes | Serves 10

- 120 ml honey
- 3 tablespoons butter, melted
- 1 teaspoon salt
- 475 ml sesame sticks
- 475 ml pumpkin seeds
- 475 ml granola
- 235 ml cashews
- 475 ml crispy corn puff cereal
- 475 ml mini pretzel crisps

1. In a bowl, combine the honey, butter, and salt.
2. In another bowl, mix the sesame sticks, pumpkin seeds, granola, cashews, corn puff cereal, and pretzel crisps.
3. Combine the contents of the two bowls. Put the mixture in half into the two air fryer drawers and air fry at 190°C for 10 to 12 minutes to toast the snack mixture, shaking the drawers frequently.
4. Put the snack mix on a cookie sheet and allow it to cool fully.
5. Serve immediately.

Mushroom and Green Bean Casserole

Prep time: 10 minutes | Cook time: 15 minutes | Serves 4

- 4 tablespoons unsalted butter
- 60 ml diced brown onion
- 120 ml chopped white mushrooms
- 120 ml double cream
- 30 g full fat soft white cheese
- 120 ml chicken broth
- ¼ teaspoon xanthan gum
- 450 g fresh green beans, edges trimmed
- 14 g pork crackling, finely ground

1. In a medium skillet over medium heat, melt the butter. Sauté the onion and mushrooms until they become soft and fragrant, about 3 to 5 minutes.
2. Add the double cream, soft white cheese, and broth to the pan. Whisk until smooth.
3. Bring to a boil and then reduce to a simmer.
4. Sprinkle the xanthan gum into the pan and remove from heat.
5. Chop the green beans into 2-inch pieces and place into a baking dish.
6. Pour the sauce mixture over them and stir until coated. Top the dish with minced pork crackling.
7. Put the dish into the zone 1 air fryer drawer and bake at 160°C for 15 minutes. Top will be golden and green beans fork-tender when fully cooked.
8. Serve warm.

Hasselback Potatoes

Prep time: 5 minutes | Cook time: 50 minutes | Serves 4

- 4 russet or Maris Piper potatoes, peeled
- Salt and freshly ground black pepper, to taste
- 60 ml grated Parmesan cheese
- Cooking spray

1. Spray the zone 1 air fryer drawer lightly with cooking spray.
2. Make thin parallel cuts into each potato, ⅛-inch to ¼-inch apart, stopping at about ½ of the way through. The potato needs to stay intact along the bottom.
3. Spray the potatoes with cooking spray and use the hands or a silicone brush to completely coat the potatoes lightly in oil.
4. Put the potatoes, sliced side up, in the zone 1 air fryer drawer in a single layer. Leave a little room between each potato. Sprinkle the potatoes lightly with salt and black pepper. Air fry at 200°C for 20 minutes.
5. Reposition the potatoes and spritz lightly with cooking spray again. Air fry until the potatoes are fork-tender and crispy and browned, another 20 to 30 minutes.
6. Sprinkle the potatoes with Parmesan cheese and serve.

Mexican Pizza

Prep time: 10 minutes | Cook time: 7 to 9 minutes | Serves 4

- 180 ml refried beans
- 120 ml salsa
- 10 frozen precooked beef meatballs, thawed and sliced
- 1 jalapeño pepper, sliced
- 4 wholemeal pitta breads
- 235 ml shredded pepper Jack or Monterey Jack cheese
- 120 ml shredded Colby or Gouda cheese
- 80 ml sour cream

1. In a medium bowl, combine the refried beans, salsa, meatballs, and jalapeño pepper.
2. Top the pittas with the refried bean mixture and sprinkle with the cheeses.
3. Place into the zone 1 drawer. Select Bake button and adjust temperature to 190°C, set time to 8 to 10 minutes and press Start.
4. Until the pizza is crisp and the cheese is melted and starts to brown, top each pizza with a dollop of sour cream and serve warm.

Teriyaki Prawn Skewers

Prep time: 10 minutes | Cook time: 6 minutes | Serves 6

- 1½ tablespoons mirin
- 1½ teaspoons ginger paste
- 1½ tablespoons soy sauce
- 12 large prawns, peeled and deveined
- 1 large egg
- 180 ml panko breadcrumbs
- Cooking spray

1. Combine the mirin, ginger paste, and soy sauce in a large bowl. Stir to mix well.
2. Dunk the prawns in the bowl of mirin mixture, then wrap the bowl in plastic and refrigerate for 1 hour to marinate.
3. Spritz the air fryer drawer with cooking spray. Run twelve 4-inch skewers through each prawn.
4. Whisk the egg in the bowl of marinade to combine well. Pour the breadcrumbs on a plate. Dredge the prawn skewers in the egg mixture, then shake the excess off and roll over the breadcrumbs to coat well.
5. Put the prawn skewers half in zone 1, the remaining in zone 2 and spritz with cooking spray.
6. In zone 1, select Air fry button, adjust temperature to 200°C, set time to 6 minutes.
7. In zone 2, select Match Cook and press Start. Flip the prawn skewers halfway through.
8. Until the prawns are opaque and firm, remove and serve immediately.

Thick-Crust Pepperoni Pizza

Prep time: 5 minutes | Cook time: 10 minutes | Serves 2

- 10 ounces purchased fresh pizza dough (not pre-baked)
- Olive oil spray
- ¼ cup purchased pizza sauce
- 10 slices pepperoni
- ⅓ cup grated Italian cheese blend

1. Preheat the oven to 220°C/200°C fan/gas mark 7.
2. Generously coat the inside of a 6-inch round cake pan for a small oven, a 7-inch round cake pan for a medium oven, or an 8-inch round cake pan for a large oven with olive oil spray.
3. Set the dough in the pan and press it to fill the bottom in an even, thick layer. Spread the sauce over the dough, then top with the pepperoni and cheese.
4. Bake for 10-12 minutes or until the crust is puffed, brown, and bubbling.
5. Use kitchen tongs to transfer the cake pan to a wire rack. Cool for only a minute or so. Use a spatula to loosen the pizza from the pan and lift it out and onto the rack. Continue cooling for a few minutes before cutting into wedges to serve.

Air Fried Blistered Tomatoes

Prep time: 5 minutes | Cook time: 10 minutes | Serves 4 to 6

- 900 g cherry tomatoes
- 2 tablespoons olive oil
- 2 teaspoons balsamic vinegar
- ½ teaspoon salt
- ½ teaspoon ground black pepper

1. Toss the cherry tomatoes with olive oil in a large bowl to coat well.
2. Pour the tomatoes in a cake pan. Put the cake pan into the zone 1 drawer. Air fry the cherry tomatoes at 200°C for 10 minutes or until the tomatoes are blistered and lightly wilted.
3. Shake the drawer halfway through. Transfer the blistered tomatoes to a large bowl and toss with balsamic vinegar, salt, and black pepper before serving.

Honey Glazed BBQ Pork Ribs

Prep time: 15 minutes | Cook time: 26 minutes | Serves 4

- 900g pork ribs
- 85g honey, divided
- 240g BBQ sauce
- ½ teaspoon garlic powder
- 2 tablespoons tomato ketchup
- 1 tablespoon Worcestershire sauce
- 1 tablespoon low-sodium soy sauce
- Freshly ground white pepper, as required

1. In a bowl, mix together honey and the remaining ingredients except pork ribs.
2. Add the pork ribs and coat with the mixture generously.
3. Refrigerate to marinate for about 20 minutes.
4. Grease basket of Ninja Foodi 2-Basket Air Fryer.
5. Press your chosen zone - "Zone 1" or "Zone 2" and then rotate the knob to select "Air Fry".
6. Set the temperature to 180 degrees C and then set the time for 5 minutes to preheat.
7. After preheating, arrange the ribs into the basket of each zone.
8. Slide the basket into the Air Fryer and set the time for 26 minutes.
9. While cooking, flip the ribs once halfway through.
10. After cooking time is completed, remove the ribs from Air Fryer and place onto serving plates.
11. Drizzle with the remaining honey and serve immediately.

Classic Churros

Prep time: 35 minutes | Cook time: 10 minutes per batch | Serves 8

- 4 tablespoons butter
- ¼ teaspoon salt
- 120 ml water
- 120 ml plain flour
- 2 large eggs
- 2 teaspoons ground cinnamon
- 60 ml granulated white sugar
- Cooking spray

1. Put the butter, salt, and water in a saucepan. Bring to a boil until the butter is melted on high heat.
2. Keep stirring. Reduce the heat to medium and fold in the flour to form a dough.
3. Keep cooking and stirring until the dough is dried out and coat the pan with a crust.
4. Turn off the heat and scrape the dough in a large bowl. Allow to cool for 15 minutes.
5. Break and whisk the eggs into the dough with a hand mixer until the dough is sanity and firm enough to shape.
6. Scoop up 1 tablespoon of the dough and roll it into a ½-inch-diameter and 2-inch-long cylinder.
7. Repeat with remaining dough to make 12 cylinders in total.
8. Combine the cinnamon and sugar in a large bowl and dunk the cylinders into the cinnamon mix to coat. Arrange the cylinders on a plate and refrigerate for 20 minutes.
9. Spritz the two air fryer drawers with cooking spray. Place the cylinders in half into the two air fryer drawers and spritz with cooking spray. Air fry at 190°C for 10 minutes or until golden brown and fluffy. Flip them halfway through.
10. Serve immediately.

Fried Dill Pickles with Buttermilk Dressing

Prep time: 45 minutes | Cook time: 8 minutes | Serves 6 to 8

- Buttermilk Dressing:
- 60 ml buttermilk
- 60 ml chopped spring onions
- 180 ml mayonnaise
- 120 ml sour cream
- ½ teaspoon cayenne pepper
- ½ teaspoon onion powder
- ½ teaspoon garlic powder
- 1 tablespoon chopped chives
- 2 tablespoons chopped fresh dill
- Rock salt and ground black pepper, to taste
- Fried Dill Pickles:
- 180 ml plain flour
- 1 (900 g) jar kosher dill pickles, cut into 4 spears, drained
- 600 ml panko breadcrumbs
- 2 eggs, beaten with 2 tablespoons water
- Rock salt and ground black pepper, to taste
- Cooking spray

1. Combine the ingredients for the dressing in a bowl. Stir to mix well.
2. Wrap the bowl in plastic and refrigerate for 30 minutes or until ready to serve.
3. Pour the flour in a bowl and sprinkle with salt and ground black pepper. Stir to mix well.
4. Put the breadcrumbs in a separate bowl.
5. Pour the beaten eggs in a third bowl.
6. Dredge the pickle spears in the flour, then into the eggs, and then into the panko to coat well. Shake the excess off.
7. Arrange the pickle spears in a single layer in the two air fryer drawers and spritz with cooking spray. Air fry at 200°C for 8 minutes.
8. Flip the pickle spears halfway through. Serve the pickle spears with buttermilk dressing.

Prawns with Sriracha and Worcestershire Sauce

Prep time: 15 minutes | Cook time: 10 minutes per batch | Serves 4

- 1 tablespoon Sriracha sauce
- 1 teaspoon Worcestershire sauce
- 2 tablespoons sweet chilli sauce
- 180 ml mayonnaise
- 1 egg, beaten
- 235 ml panko breadcrumbs
- 450 g raw prawns, shelled and deveined, rinsed and drained
- Lime wedges, for serving
- Cooking spray

1. Spritz the two air fryer drawers with cooking spray.
2. Combine the Sriracha sauce, Worcestershire sauce, chilli sauce, and mayo in a bowl. Stir to mix well.
3. Reserve 80 ml the mixture as the dipping sauce. Combine the remaining sauce mixture with the beaten egg. Stir to mix well.
4. Put the panko in a separate bowl.
5. Dredge the prawns in the sauce mixture first, then into the panko. Roll the prawns to coat well. Shake the excess off.
6. Place the prawns in half into the two air fryer drawers, then spritz with cooking spray. Air fry the prawns at 180°C for 10 minutes or until opaque. Flip the prawns halfway through the cooking time.
7. Remove the prawns from the air fryer and serve with reserve sauce mixture and squeeze the lime wedges over.

Simple Lamb Meatballs

Prep time: 10 minutes | Cook time: 12 minutes | Serves 4

- 455g lamb mince
- 1 teaspoon ground cinnamon
- 1 teaspoon ground cumin
- 2 teaspoons granulated onion
- 2 tablespoons fresh parsley
- Salt and black pepper, to taste

1. Add lamb mince, onion, cinnamon, cumin, parsley, salt and pepper in a large bowl. Mix until well combined.
2. Make 2.5cm balls from the mixture and set aside.
3. Grease basket of Ninja Foodi 2-Basket Air Fryer.
4. Press your chosen zone - "Zone 1" or "Zone 2" and then rotate the knob to select "Air Fry".
5. Set the temperature to 195 degrees C and then set the time for 5 minutes to preheat.
6. After preheating, arrange the meatballs into the basket of each zone.
7. Slide the basket into the Air Fryer and set the time for 12 minutes.
8. Flip the meatballs once halfway through.
9. Take out and serve warm.

Golden Nuggets

Prep time: 15 minutes | Cook time: 4 minutes per batch | Serves 6 to 8

- 235 ml plain flour, plus more for dusting
- 1 teaspoon baking powder
- ½ teaspoon butter, at room temperature, plus more for brushing
- ¼ teaspoon salt
- 60 ml water
- ⅛ teaspoon onion powder
- ¼ teaspoon garlic powder
- ⅛ teaspoon seasoning salt
- Cooking spray

1. Line the two air fryer drawers with parchment paper.
2. Mix the flour, baking powder, butter, and salt in a large bowl. Stir to mix well. Gradually whisk in the water until a sanity dough forms.
3. Put the dough on a lightly floured work surface, then roll it out into a ½-inch thick rectangle with a rolling pin.
4. Cut the dough into about twenty 1- or 2-inch squares, then arrange the squares in a single layer in the two air fryer drawers. Spritz with cooking spray.
5. Combine onion powder, garlic powder, and seasoning salt in a small bowl. Stir to mix well, then sprinkle the squares with the powder mixture. Air fry the dough squares at
6. 190°C for 4 minutes or until golden brown. Flip the squares halfway through the cooking time.
7. Remove the golden nuggets from the air fryer and brush with more butter immediately.
8. Serve warm.

Air Fried Spicy Olives

Prep time: 10 minutes | Cook time: 5 minutes | Serves 4

- 340 g pitted black extra-large olives
- 60 ml plain flour
- 235 ml panko breadcrumbs
- 2 teaspoons dried thyme
- 1 teaspoon red pepper flakes
- 1 teaspoon smoked paprika
- 1 egg beaten with 1 tablespoon water
- Vegetable oil for spraying

1. Drain the olives and place them on a paper towel-lined plate to dry.
2. Put the flour on a plate.
3. Combine the panko, thyme, red pepper flakes, and paprika on a separate plate.
4. Dip an olive in the flour, shaking off any excess, then coat with egg mixture. Dredge the olive in the panko mixture, pressing to make the crumbs adhere, and place the breaded olive on a platter.
5. Repeat with the remaining olives.
6. Spray the olives with oil and place them in a single layer in half into the two air fryer drawers. Air fry at 200°C for 5 minutes until the breading is browned and crispy.
7. Serve warm

Cinnamon Rolls with Cream Glaze

Prep time: 2 hours 15 minutes | Cook time: 10 minutes | Serves 8

- 450 g frozen bread dough, thawed
- 2 tablespoons melted butter
- 1½ tablespoons cinnamon
- 180 ml brown sugar
- Cooking spray
- Cream Glaze:
- 110 g soft white cheese
- ½ teaspoon vanilla extract
- 2 tablespoons melted butter
- 300 ml powdered erythritol

1. Place the bread dough on a clean work surface, then roll the dough out into a rectangle with a rolling pin.
2. Brush the top of the dough with melted butter and leave 1-inch edges uncovered.
3. Combine the cinnamon and sugar in a small bowl, then sprinkle the dough with the cinnamon mixture.
4. Roll the dough over tightly, then cut the dough log into 8 portions. Wrap the portions in plastic, better separately, and let sit to rise for 1 or 2 hours.
5. Meanwhile, combine the ingredients for the glaze in a separate small bowl. Stir to mix well.
6. Spritz the two air fryer drawers with cooking spray. Transfer the risen rolls in half into the two air fryer drawer. Air fry at 180°C for 5 minutes or until golden brown. Flip the rolls halfway through.
7. Serve the rolls with the glaze.

Cajun Flank Steak

Prep time: 10 minutes | Cook time: 7 minutes | Serves 4

- 900g flank steak
- 1 Cajun seasoning
- ½ teaspoon smoked paprika
- Salt, to taste

1. Grease either basket of "Zone 1" or "Zone 2" of Ninja Foodi 2-Basket Air Fryer.
2. Press your chosen zone - "Zone 1" or "Zone 2" and then rotate the knob for the zone to select "Bake".
3. Set the temperature to 215 degrees C and then set the time for 5 minutes to preheat.
4. Rub the steaks with Cajun seasoning evenly.
5. After preheating, arrange steak into the basket.
6. Slide basket into Air Fryer and set the time for 7 minutes.
7. After cooking time is completed, remove the steak from Air Fryer and set aside to cool.
8. Slice and serve.

Jewish Blintzes

Prep time: 5 minutes | Cook time: 10 minutes | Serves 8

- 2 (213 g) packages farmer or ricotta cheese, mashed
- 60 ml soft white cheese
- ¼ teaspoon vanilla extract
- 60 ml granulated white sugar
- 8 egg roll wrappers
- 4 tablespoons butter, melted

1. Combine the cheese, soft white cheese, vanilla extract, and sugar in a bowl. Stir to mix well.
2. Unfold the egg roll wrappers on a clean work surface, spread 60 ml filling at the edge of each wrapper and leave a ½-inch edge uncovering.
3. Wet the edges of the wrappers with water and fold the uncovered edge over the filling. Fold the left and right sides in the centre, then tuck the edge under the filling and fold to wrap the filling.
4. Brush the wrappers with melted butter, then arrange the wrappers in a single layer in the two air fryer drawers, seam side down. Leave a little space between each two wrappers. Air fry at 190°C for 10 minutes or until golden brown.
5. Serve immediately.

Kale Salad Sushi Rolls with Sriracha Mayonnaise

Prep time: 10 minutes | Cook time: 10 minutes | Serves 12

- Kale Salad:
- 350 ml chopped kale
- 1 tablespoon sesame seeds
- ¾ teaspoon soy sauce
- ¾ teaspoon toasted sesame oil
- ½ teaspoon rice vinegar
- ¼ teaspoon ginger
- ⅛ teaspoon garlic powder
- Sushi Rolls:
- 3 sheets sushi nori
- 1 batch cauliflower rice
- ½ avocado, sliced
- Sriracha Mayonnaise:
- 60 ml Sriracha sauce
- 60 ml vegan mayonnaise
- Coating:
- 120 ml panko breadcrumbs

1. In a medium bowl, toss all the ingredients for the salad together until well coated and set aside.
2. Place a sheet of nori on a clean work surface and spread the cauliflower rice in an even layer on the nori. Scoop 2 to 3 tablespoon of kale salad on the rice and spread over. Place 1 or 2 avocado slices on top.
3. Roll up the sushi, pressing gently to get a nice, tight roll.
4. Repeat to make the remaining 2 rolls.
5. In a bowl, stir together the Sriracha sauce and mayonnaise until smooth.
6. Add breadcrumbs to a separate bowl.
7. Dredge the sushi rolls in Sriracha Mayonnaise, then roll in breadcrumbs till well coated.
8. Place the coated sushi rolls in the two air fryer drawers and air fry at 200°C for 10 minutes, or until golden brown and crispy. Flip the sushi rolls gently halfway through to ensure even cooking.
9. Transfer to a platter and rest for 5 minutes before slicing each roll into 8 pieces. Serve warm.

Appendix 1 Measurement Conversion Chart

Volume Equivalents (Dry)	
US STANDARD	METRIC (APPROXIMATE)
1/8 teaspoon	0.5 mL
1/4 teaspoon	1 mL
1/2 teaspoon	2 mL
3/4 teaspoon	4 mL
1 teaspoon	5 mL
1 tablespoon	15 mL
1/4 cup	59 mL
1/2 cup	118 mL
3/4 cup	177 mL
1 cup	235 mL
2 cups	475 mL
3 cups	700 mL
4 cups	1 L

Volume Equivalents (Liquid)		
US STANDARD	US STANDARD (OUNCES)	METRIC (APPROXIMATE)
2 tablespoons	1 fl.oz.	30 mL
1/4 cup	2 fl.oz.	60 mL
1/2 cup	4 fl.oz.	120 mL
1 cup	8 fl.oz.	240 mL
1 1/2 cup	12 fl.oz.	355 mL
2 cups or 1 pint	16 fl.oz.	475 mL
4 cups or 1 quart	32 fl.oz.	1 L
1 gallon	128 fl.oz.	4 L

Temperatures Equivalents	
FAHRENHEIT(F)	CELSIUS(C) APPROXIMATE)
225 °F	107 °C
250 °F	120 ° °C
275 °F	135 °C
300 °F	150 °C
325 °F	160 °C
350 °F	180 °C
375 °F	190 °C
400 °F	205 °C
425 °F	220 °C
450 °F	235 °C
475 °F	245 °C
500 °F	260 °C

Weight Equivalents	
US STANDARD	METRIC (APPROXIMATE)
1 ounce	28 g
2 ounces	57 g
5 ounces	142 g
10 ounces	284 g
15 ounces	425 g
16 ounces (1 pound)	455 g
1.5 pounds	680 g
2 pounds	907 g

Appendix 2 The Dirty Dozen and Clean Fifteen

The Environmental Working Group (EWG) is a nonprofit, nonpartisan organization dedicated to protecting human health and the environment Its mission is to empower people to live healthier lives in a healthier environment. This organization publishes an annual list of the twelve kinds of produce, in sequence, that have the highest amount of pesticide residue-the Dirty Dozen-as well as a list of the fifteen kinds of produce that have the least amount of pesticide residue-the Clean Fifteen.

THE DIRTY DOZEN

The 2016 Dirty Dozen includes the following produce. These are considered among the year's most important produce to buy organic:

Strawberries	Spinach
Apples	Tomatoes
Nectarines	Bell peppers
Peaches	Cherry tomatoes
Celery	Cucumbers
Grapes	Kale/collard greens
Cherries	Hot peppers

The Dirty Dozen list contains two additional itemskale/collard greens and hot peppers-because they tend to contain trace levels of highly hazardous pesticides.

THE CLEAN FIFTEEN

The least critical to buy organically are the Clean Fifteen list. The following are on the 2016 list:

Avocados	Papayas
Corn	Kiw
Pineapples	Eggplant
Cabbage	Honeydew
Sweet peas	Grapefruit
Onions	Cantaloupe
Asparagus	Cauliflower
Mangos	

Some of the sweet corn sold in the United States are made from genetically engineered (GE) seedstock. Buy organic varieties of these crops to avoid GE produce.

Appendix 3 Index

A
all-purpose flour 50, 53
allspice 15
almond 5, 14
ancho chile 10
ancho chile powder 5
apple 9
apple cider vinegar 9
arugula 51
avocado 11

B
bacon 52
balsamic vinegar 7, 12, 52
basil 5, 8, 11, 13
beet 52
bell pepper 50, 51, 53
black beans 50, 51
broccoli 51, 52, 53
buns 52
butter 50

C
canola oil 50, 51, 52
carrot 52, 53
cauliflower 5, 52
cayenne 5, 52
cayenne pepper 52
Cheddar cheese 52
chicken 6
chili powder 50, 51
chipanle pepper 50
chives 5, 6, 52
cinnamon 15
coconut 6
Colby Jack cheese 51
coriander 52
corn 50, 51
corn kernels 50
cumin 5, 10, 15, 50, 51, 52

D
diced panatoes 50
Dijon mustard 7, 12, 13, 51
dry onion powder 52

E
egg 14, 50, 53
enchilada sauce 51

F
fennel seed 53
flour 50, 53
fresh chives 5, 6, 52
fresh cilantro 52
fresh cilantro leaves 52
fresh dill 5
fresh parsley 6, 52
fresh parsley leaves 52

G
garlic 5, 9, 10, 11, 13, 14, 50, 51, 52, 53
garlic powder 8, 9, 52, 53

H
half-and-half 50
hemp seeds 8
honey 9, 51

I
instant rice 51

K
kale 14
kale leaves 14
ketchup 53
kosher salt 5, 10, 15

L
lemon 5, 6, 14, 51, 53
lemon juice 6, 8, 11, 13, 14, 51
lime 9, 12
lime juice 9, 12
lime zest 9, 12

M
maple syrup 7, 12, 53
Marinara Sauce 5
micro greens 52
milk 5, 50
mixed berries 12
Mozzarella 50, 53
Mozzarella cheese 50, 53
mushroom 51, 52
mustard 51, 53
mustard powder 53

N

nutritional yeast 5

O

olive oil 5, 12, 13, 14, 50, 51, 52, 53
onion 5, 50, 51
onion powder 8
oregano 5, 8, 10, 50

P

panatoes 50, 52
paprika 5, 15, 52
Parmesan cheese 51, 53
parsley 6, 52
pesto 52
pink Himalayan salt 5, 7, 8, 11
pizza dough 50, 53
pizza sauce 50
plain coconut yogurt 6
plain Greek yogurt 5
porcini powder 53
potato 53

R

Ranch dressing 52
raw honey 9, 12, 13
red pepper flakes 5, 8, 14, 15, 51, 53
ricotta cheese 53

S

saffron 52
Serrano pepper 53
sugar 10
summer squash 51

T

tahini 5, 8, 9, 11
thyme 50
toasted almonds 14
tomato 5, 50, 52, 53
turmeric 15

U

unsalted butter 50
unsweetened almond milk 5

V

vegetable broth 50
vegetable stock 51

W

white wine 8, 11
wine vinegar 8, 10, 11

Y

yogurt 5, 6

Z

zucchini 50, 51, 52, 53

SARA T. JONES

Printed in Great Britain
by Amazon